CHRISTIANITY AND PARADOX

RONALD W. HEPBURN

CHRISTIANITY AND PARADOX

Critical Studies in
Twentieth-Century
Theology

WATTS
40 Drury Lane, London, W.C.2

First published in 1958
by C. A. Watts & Co Ltd,
40 Drury Lane, London, W.C.2

Printed in Great Britain
in 12 pt. Fournier type
by Richard Clay & Co Ltd
Bungay, Suffolk

CONTENTS

ACKNOWLEDGEMENTS

I am indebted to a great many friends of widely differing philosophical and religious persuasions for help and encouragement in tackling the problems with which the following studies are concerned. To name them all would be impossible. Two, however, cry out to be mentioned. One is the head of the department in which I teach, Professor D. M. MacKinnon, whose deep interest in, and knowledge of, contemporary theology can surely be matched by few British philosophers to-day. The other is Professor Antony Flew, who gave generously of his time and logical skill in helping me to clarify and improve both argument and exposition at many points.

I am grateful to the following publishers for permission to quote certain passages: to Messrt T. & T. Clark for *Church Dogmatics*, by Karl Barth, and *I and Thou* by Martin Buber; to the Lutterworth Press for *Essays in Christology for Karl Barth*, by D.M. MacKinnon; to James Nisbet & Company for *The World and God*, by H. H. Farmer; and to the S.C.M. Press for *The Divine–Human Encounter*, by Emil Brunner, *Christian Apologetics*, by Alan Richardson, and *A Theological Word Book of the Bible*.

CHAPTER ONE
CONTEMPORARY PHILOSOPHY AND CHRISTIAN APOLOGETICS

———

I HAVE subtitled the following essays *'critical* studies in twentieth-century theology', in order to make it clear that they do not contain a constructive, positive contribution to Christian apologetics. They argue, on the contrary, that a number of influential theological views, believed by their authors to be well defended against the criticisms of contemporary philosophers, are not so defended, but are exposed to a variety of logical objections which render them untenable—or at least less sure than their upholders believe. On the other hand, these studies are not negative polemic with a purely destructive, iconoclastic purpose. They would not, in the first place, have been written but for my personal pilgrimage in search of a satisfactory justification of religious belief. And this is a *continuing* pilgrimage, despite the fact that none of the approaches discussed in this book seems to me to survive scrutiny. Second, the studies attempt more than negative criticism, in that they seek to bring out how a theology may be logically faulty but yet express insights of enduring value concerning human experience, and thus still be worth study by sceptics as well as believers, for all their differences over the interpretation of those experiences.

But, at the same time, the wide extent of the logical breakdowns themselves prompts further serious questions that cannot be shirked; for instance, the question how can one live in religious uncertainty, if one has what might be called a 'naturally religious mind'? And if one finds oneself unable to make sense of the idea that God is the author of all values, can one retain one's moral seriousness or still be sure that 'life has a meaning' or is 'worthwhile'?

If these are problems which the sceptic will find more urgent than the Christian, that does not mean that this book is addressed only to the former. It aims, in fact, to present a challenge to the theologians whose views it discusses—to suggest that they have tended radically to underestimate the grave logical difficulties in giving meaning to religious language, difficulties spotlighted by recent linguistic philosophy; and to suggest that before they can make good their claim that religious language is genuinely meaningful, they may have yet to go through a much darker 'night of the intellect' than they have realized.

I

First of all, it may well be asked what right has a philosopher to intrude into the theologian's domain at all? Has he any more authority to judge a theological system (in his capacity as philosopher) than a plumber has to judge a mathematical system or a physicist a string quartet, in *their* professional capacities? The philosopher and the theologian, however, are related more closely than these comparisons would imply. For the theologian is himself philosopher in so far as he attempts at all a logical scrutiny of the concepts he constantly uses. He is philosopher when he speaks of the special sorts of ways religious language works— through 'symbols', 'analogies', 'parables'; or of how like and how unlike knowledge of God is from knowledge of human beings; or when he discriminates among accounts of morality, seeing religious implications in one, and judging another incompatible with Christian belief.

He may, of course, dodge these and the like questions; he may even convince himself that they do not arise within his sort of theology. But suppose someone challenges that claim to theological independence and recalls the theologian to the task of showing how his technical terms are related to the language of the market-place, or seeks to know on what grounds he calls one paradox a 'palpable contradiction in terms' and another a 'sublime mystery of faith'. The person who does that, even if by profession a philosopher, is surely both continuing a theological discussion and opening a philosophical one at the same moment. As philosopher, he will bring to his inquiry what insights, distinctions, methods of clarification he has found generally useful in sifting straight from crooked thinking. What these methods will be like, and how helpful they will be with theological problems will naturally vary according to the brand of philosophy he practises. What *cannot* justly be said is that the philosopher comes to theological discussion as an alien and impertinent interloper.

The philosophical style that prevails in much of this book is one with which few Christian theologians are at ease; that only recently some of them have come to distinguish from its ancestor, logical positivism. I call it a 'style', for it cannot be counted a school, nor has it even a single acceptable name—'the philosophy of language', 'linguistic analysis' are perhaps its commonest nicknames. It is a philosophy of many strands, in which no party dogmas are held by all practitioners.

It is no simple matter to understand the theologian's embarrassment at the philosophy of language. It is true that it shares with logical positivism a distrust of speculation, a reluctance to proceed far from the checks upon sense and sanity that everyday language provides. But in this it is not obviously the enemy of theology. For a great many theologians have recently been equally vociferous against the perils of speculation within their own sphere. Again, the philosophy of language inherits from Hume a respect for 'experience'—an empiricist slant. But some theologians too have even espoused a kind of theological empiricism. If philosophy in the thirties could dismiss religious assertions as 'nonsense' because they cannot be verified by observation, some of their mid-century counterparts can be heard saying tolerantly,

'Every sort of statement has its own sort of logic.' May not religious statements have a peculiar, but valid, logic of their own? And how can the philosophy of language be seen as a threat to theology, when not a few of its exponents are themselves reflective Christians, and find their philosophy a useful critical tool in interpreting and clarifying their faith?

2

Yet I think the theologian's uneasiness is largely justified, despite what has just been said: and this for four reasons at least.

(i) Linguistic philosophy has restated and immensely sharpened the attack on traditional arguments for the existence of God. To a large extent, this consists of a developing of arguments deployed originally by Hume, notably in his *Dialogues Concerning Natural Religion*. To mention only two examples: the 'ontological argument' maintained that from a scrutiny of the very *notion* of God the fact of his existence could be deduced. More accurately, if one were to specify fully the perfections of which God's nature must be composed, the perfection of existence could not be left out. Against this Hume argued that there *could* be no concept with this extraordinary characteristic, a concept of a being that *has to exist*. It is always possible, he held, with any concept whatever 'to conceive the non-existence of what we formerly conceived to exist';[1] or (as Professor G. E. Moore has put it in our own time) that 'existence is not a predicate' like roughness or heaviness. The closely related 'cosmological argument' set God apart from every 'contingent' being, from every being, that is, which happens to exist and might equally well happen *not* to exist. God must be above all happening: his being, and his alone, must be 'necessary'.

[1] *Dialogues Concerning Natural Religion*, ed. Kemp Smith (London: Nelson, 1947), p. 189. Cf. Kant, *Critique of Pure Reason*, ed. Kemp Smith (London: Macmillan, 1950), pp. 500 ff.

Most contemporary logicians (again drawing on Humean distinctions) insist that where necessity is in fact achieved by an assertion, it is only at the high cost of ceasing to say anything, by means of that assertion, about the world. Examples are the necessary truths of logic and mathematics, which are guaranteed true through the conventions of our symbolism. This view of necessity is of course contested by some theologians, and in Chapter Ten we shall examine some of their efforts to construe it differently—efforts that so far seem unsuccessful, although interesting.

The philosopher of language looks back to Hume and Kant once more in the recent criticism he has been offering of the First Cause argument and its relatives. It may be briefly summarized as follows. We use the word 'cause' in ordinary contexts to express the relation in which certain events in the world stand to other events. We teach it by drawing attention to groups of events suitably related. But, since this is the 'home' of its use in the language, it is by no means sure that we know what we are saying when we speak of something or someone (*not* in the world) 'causing' the world as a whole to come into being, or 'maintaining' it in being. Or again, compare these sentences—'Outside my room a sparrow is chirping', 'Outside the city the speed limit ends', 'Outside the earth's atmosphere meteors do not burn out', and finally 'God is outside the universe, outside space and time'. What of this last statement? The word 'outside' gets its central meaning from relating item to item *within* the universe. It too is being stretched to breaking-point in being applied to the whole universe as related to some being that is not-the-universe: its sense is being extended to the point where we may easily come to speak nonsense without noticing it, since the phrases 'cause of the universe' and 'outside the universe' are certainly still *grammatically*, though perhaps no longer logically, in order.

(ii) In all this, some Protestant theologians will say, 'I and the linguistic philosopher are allies, not enemies. For theology too has seen the barrenness and deceptiveness of natural religion, and joins hands with any sceptic who denies that the God of Christianity can be proved to exist by unaided reason.' Whether he turn to 'biblical theology', or dramatizes faith as a 'leap in the dark' beyond rational justification, or stakes all on his sense of direct encounter with God as the *Thou* of prayer; in each case he turns his back simultaneously on traditional natural religion. He either abandons the old arguments for God altogether, or sees them (like Paul Tillich) as expressions only of the *problems* to which revealed religion provides the answers.

But is it true that appealing to revelation makes a theology immune to any further logical or philosophical criticism? A great many influential theologians seem to believe that it does. They see philosophy as confined to study of the arguments of natural theology, having no right to enter the charmed circle of revealed religion, that circle in which the biblical ideas and images, the biblical notion even of *truth*, have (they claim) unchallengeable authority.

I believe that today it requires to be said firmly and repeatedly that this is an enormous, costly illusion: that the insights gained by recent philosophy, so far from *diminishing* the need for rational inquiry within theology, have vastly *increased* that need. They have increased it by showing that one critical question about any kind of religious language is not whether its claims can be established by this or that argument, but whether they have been given a coherent *meaning*, a consistent use. And *this* is a question that remains critical as long as these concepts are employed in any discourse whatever, even if it does appear under the heading, 'Revealed Religion' or 'Dogmatics', rather than 'Natural Religion'. If God is said to be 'Father', 'Creator', and if it turns out that these statements lack meaning; if we find on examination that all the normal sense of those familiar words has been whittled away in the attempt to set them aside from a secular to a sacred use, then it makes no difference whether this is backed up by appeal to reason or to revelation.

If the theologian is to communicate at all, he must establish

6

some sort of contact-points between his special senses of the words he uses and the ordinary senses of these words. If he has modified their meanings in using them to speak of God, he must show clearly the direction in which the modification has taken place. He must convince us, too, that the change of meaning is not so drastic as to erode away the entire sense the words originally possessed. The search for these contact-points and the general inquiry into meaningfulness certainly deserve to be counted as vital parts of the apologetic task today, a task the magnitude of which is as yet realized by very few theologians.

(iii) Theology is justified in its uneasiness at the philosophy of language, thirdly, because of the partial success of what can be called its 'therapeutic' efforts. A number of chronically vexing philosophical enigmas, dilemmas, paradoxes has recently been shown to result, not from any mystery in the nature of things, not from some irremediable limitation of our intellectual powers, but from sheer misunderstandings of the logic of our language. Words that we can perfectly well handle in everyday contexts play tricks with us when we employ them to describe matters of very high generality or abstraction. Like some substances at very low temperatures, they behave in unexpected and abnormal ways. Nevertheless, once these vagaries of language are carefully mapped and studied, what looked like a philosophical mystery is shown to have been a muddle instead. A philosopher who believes he has taken the paradox out of, say, the freewill-determinism dilemma and reconciled our claim to know the minds of others with the fact that we see and touch only their bodies,[1] such a philosopher cannot be blamed for assuming a militant attitude to yet unresolved paradoxes, and seeing them as candidates for dissolution rather than as exhibits for a museum of metaphysical marvels. It is not to be wondered that the theologian finds him disquieting company.

[1] Whether or not these particular problems have yielded or not to this approach is irrelevant to my present point—the description of the attitude of mind with which such a philosopher will approach theological paradoxes.

For the theologian has no wish to allow the mysteries of divinity, the irreducible paradoxes in all our talk about God, to be made over merely as balloons for the philosophical pin.

The theologian, however, retaliates by accusing the philosopher of being after all, a speculator, a metaphysician, in disguise. 'You hold', he says, 'as a metaphysical dogma that *there are no mysteries*. You believe that given persistence, cleverness, and good luck, we shall be able to describe all that there *is* to describe without paradox: or (putting it the other way round) that there are no entities such that we human beings are compelled to talk about paradoxically or not at all.' But the philosopher might reply, 'No, I'm not advancing any dogma. If I find, as I *do* find, that certain long-standing puzzles have in fact yielded or begun to yield when approached with the suspicion that they *might* turn out to be confusions of language, then I think I am justified in going on to attack further paradoxes at least in the *hope* that they will yield in the same way.' 'In that case,' says the theologian, 'you are admitting, aren't you, that some paradoxes may never yield, but remain quite opaque to our understanding—just as I claim the paradoxes in all our talk about God will remain, for the most part, opaque?'

'I don't see any way of ruling that possibility out in advance,' comes the reply, 'but it is only after trying one's hardest to dissolve them and by discovering why they *resist* dissolution that one could prove them to be opaque rather than just confused.'

So the core of the problem would now seem to lie in knowing in what circumstances we should regard some stubbornly paradoxical concept as a muddle, to be dissolved sometime in the future, and when to regard it as a mystery, to be lived with and perhaps held in reverence. We shall return to this our central problem in Chapter Two.

(iv) Mid-century philosophy is taking a renewed interest in philosophical *construction*, even in some kinds of metaphysics, and has ceased simply to stigmatize these as altogether wrong-headed.[1] But once more the theologian has reason to wonder whether the conception of metaphysics that some linguistic philosophers are developing could be of much help to *him*—even if he is one of those theologians who do hanker after metaphysics of some sort. For the linguistic philosopher's metaphysics tends to be an imaginative aid to the comprehending of the familiar, not to the discovery of the unseen. It may consist in the adoption of ways of speaking, other than our normal ways, in order to throw into relief unnoticed characteristics of normal language and hence of the world it describes. Alternatively, the philosopher may imagine that the circumstances of our lives and the backcloth against which they are lived out are transformed in some important respect, while the language remains constant. Then, he asks, how would that language require to be adapted so as to cope with these imagined changes? But note again, the objective of these thought-experiments is still the better understanding of the everyday world and our everyday language. This, clearly, is not speculative metaphysics of the kind which can conclude: 'therefore God exists', or 'and so the soul is immortal'. It is true that a part of what the apologist tries to do is to re-describe the familiar from the theistic viewpoint: but he will seldom admit that this exhausts his task. And he is surely right.

3

More needs to be said about the themes of 'verification' and 'falsification' which have been so prominent in recent philosophical theology written from the linguistic standpoint. The original logical positivists held that language had three main functions: it could state facts, it could express feeling, and it could be used to calculate—to work out systems of 'necessarily true' propositions

[1] See *The Revolution in Philosophy* (London: Macmillan, 1956), pp. 97 to the end.

in logic and mathematics. Now, to which of these pigeonholes could religious and theological language be plausibly said to belong? It certainly could not belong to the last-mentioned class; for, as we have seen, to be a truth of logic involves saying nothing whatever about what is the case. Statements so informative and important as 'God exists' or 'God does not exist' cannot reasonably be taken as tautologies. If religious language is fact-stating language (the positivist went on), then there must be some observational tests that would verify these 'facts', or at least some tests that would falsify them. For fact-stating language derives its meaning from the possibility of such experimental checks. If a statement could *not* be verified *or* falsified by any imaginable test, then, whatever else it might be doing, it could not be stating a fact. But God is not a being such that we can point at him, saying, 'Lo, here!' or 'Lo, there!', or hear him or see him, or bring forward indubitable evidence from which he might be inferred. So it seemed no more plausible to say that statements about God were testable by observation or experiment and thus properly classed as fact-stating. If these two options were rejected by the positivist, only the third remained—religious language evoked emotion, expressed feeling, and nothing more. Its paradoxes and mysteries merely disguised the nonsense it really was, if considered as giving information about the world and our place in it.

And so the positivists believed they had 'eliminated' theology. But one can easily understand why many theologians were little perturbed at their boast to have done so. For it was in *scientific* language that the positivists were plainly most interested. When they denied that a fact-stating assertion could be meaningful unless there were experimental checks relevant to verifying it, this made most sense (indeed very good sense) in the context of the scientist's laboratory reports. As Sir Arthur Eddington put it, 'The meaning of a scientific statement is to be ascertained by reference to the steps which would be taken to verify it.' But they did not convince the theologian that a theory of meaning that worked reasonably well in one restricted context could be used as a sure touchstone of sense and nonsense in every other sphere. At any rate, what the positivist himself said about meaning sounded very like a piece of the metaphysics he scorned. If the positivist denied this, and said instead that his theory of meaning was a *proposal* about how we might most profitably use words like 'meaningful' and 'nonsense', then the theologian had no qualms about rejecting that proposal—as very unprofitable to *him*.

It might have been better in the long run for theology if these short ways with the positivists had not been taken as excusing theologians from any further study of the movement. To shrug off the positivist challenge to religion in this way is to underestimate its seriousness. That central challenge (the demand for verification or falsification) has been presented more recently by some philosophers not themselves positivists in the strict sense, and certainly not committed to positivistic theories of meaning, rigid and over-simplified as they were. For example, Professor Antony Flew puts the main question to the theologian in this way: How different would the world have to be before you would decide that you could not reasonably go on believing? What would have to be different? If something is being *asserted* by the believer, he argues, then something else must simultaneously be being *denied*. His statements cannot both be meaningful *and* compatible with any kind of world or any kind of experiences. What the believer says about God's love can hardly be compatible with *any* amount of pain, *any* amount of unrelieved catastrophe.[1] Now Flew suspects that those apparently highly meaningful claims that the Christian makes ('There is an all-good, all-powerful God') are in fact vacuous claims. There seem to be no circumstances, real or imaginable, which would be accepted by believers as falsifying them. ('God will always love me' is taken as compatible even with 'I, or someone I love, may contract inoperable cancer.')

[1] See the discussion 'Theology and Falsification' in *New Essays in Philosophical Theology*, edited by A. G. N. Flew and A. C. MacIntyre (London: S.C.M., 1955), pp. 96 ff.

Nevertheless, as Flew well realizes, this is not quite true of all believers. Sometimes a theologian *is* prepared to state what circumstances would falsify his beliefs, what states of affairs would count decisively against them and make it irrational for him to go on believing. The value of this modified verification-challenge is precisely this, that it forces a theologian to expose the very nerve of his position, to become clear with himself (and to express to other people) on what his theology stands or falls. And incidentally he may discover by his very inability to do this that his theology is logically confused, or not at any point properly anchored to reality.

In any case, the linguistic philosopher, having delivered his challenge, must humbly examine any serious attempt that *is* made to say what would count against the Christian claims. The initiative must pass, temporarily at least, to the theologian. The Catholic apologist, for instance, may say that the only thing that would count decisively against the statement 'God exists' would be the non-existence of the world as a whole. *If* there exists a world (which would be difficult even for the philosopher to deny), then there must exist also a Ground and Source of its existence, namely God. To go on from there, the linguistic philosopher would naturally have to examine whatever form of the 'Cosmological Argument' the apologist was using. Everything would depend on its validity.

Other Christians have tried to meet the problem by saying that 'God exists' is not in any way verifiable or falsifiable, and yet *does* express something more than a feeling or attitude. 'God exists', 'God loves me' express 'slants' on the world, a slant like, for instance, my confidence in nature's regularity. I can neither prove nor disprove the statement 'Nature is always regular'. Even if on ten successive repetitions of an 'identical' scientific experiment I obtained ten different results, I should hesitate to say, 'Nature is no longer regular': but say instead, 'I'm no experimenter'. With religious statements too, rather than let anything count against them, rather than deny God's existence, his love etc., I may say, 'I'm blind, corrupted in my judgement by sin, unable to penetrate to the mysteries of Providence.'

This reply fails to satisfy many Christians as well as sceptics. It ignores the extent to which historical Christianity has admitted that had certain events, allegedly historical, not taken place, distinctively Christian belief *would* be falsified. 'If Christ be not raised, your faith is vain.' Pain, suffering, death *do* count against belief in God's goodness and love. The great question is whether the impact of the person of Jesus and the witness of his Church do not tip the balance back to faith, revealing more about ultimate reality than the *evils* reveal.

But even supposing we thought that these might tip back the balance, would we yet be sure that we knew what we were saying when we attributed that goodness and that love, not to a human being, not simply to Jesus of Nazareth, but to the unconditioned, infinite, eternal God? Mr. Ian Crombie took up that question in an influential article.[1] He began by denying that the meaningfulness of religious utterances is eroded away (as Flew thinks) by radical modification of everyday senses until no empirical claim is really being made. Crombie held that words like 'love' and 'goodness' retain their ordinary senses when predicated of God. We have it on the authority of Christ and his interpreters that the man who acts towards God as towards a being who loves him will be acting with complete propriety and fittingness, although he is quite unable to say what it is like *for God* to love, or to be good. But how does he deal with the problems of meaning in the word 'God' itself? For it is just the *ordinary* sense of 'God' that baffles understanding. Crombie does not return at this point to the old arguments for God's existence, or rather he does not rely on their *argumentative* force. Yet he sees, in certain of these, ways of manœuvring our thought away from ordinary experience in a particular direction that might be called the direction of the

[1] This appears (in common with statements of the two other views sketched in immediately above) in the same volume of essays. The authors of these other views are R. M. Hare and B. Mitchell.

transcendent. They make a gesture, he thinks, which lets us know, however dimly, to what or to whom we speak when we address 'God' in prayer. Even if there *is* muddled logic in arguing from the 'contingency' and instability of the world to an unchanging divine ground of being, that muddled movement of thought may help us to give 'God' a kind of shadowy sense, and redeem the word from being a mere meaningless noise. This may be enough for faith. Full verification of our religious beliefs, however, can be had only on the other side of death. In this life the evidence can never be complete.

I shall mention only two respects in which Crombie's interpretation might be held to be vulnerable. First, it might be questioned whether his 'non-argumentative' use of the traditional 'proofs' really can do what he believes it can do, without having unconsciously to ignore their logical flaws, and (momentarily at least) pretending that the arguments are sound after all.[1] Secondly, one can agree to a postponement of verification to the hereafter only if one believes it possible to speak intelligibly of such a life, only if sense can be given to the idea of 'surviving death' or of 'resurrection'. And a good deal of worried discussion has lately gone on about whether *personal identity* could survive the radical crisis of death: the debate continues.

I do not pursue these questions here; but they have been raised in order to draw one conclusion about the course of the discussion itself. It should be clear by now how fruitful a demand the falsification demand has been, when presented in such a way as to give the theologian maximum scope, freedom of play, in stating what *to him* counts for and against the faith he holds. But, once assume him to accept the demand, to answer it after his own fashion, and immediately the philosopher (unless he retires from the fray) is plunged into a discussion as much of technical theology as of philosophy. To glance at those specimen answers makes this obvious—'History verifies the Faith'; '. . . the old arguments can

[1] I have discussed this at greater length in *Metaphysical Beliefs*, written in collaboration with S. E. Toulmin and A. C. MacIntyre (S.C.M., 1957).

cope, if presented in a new way'; '. . . we shall know fully here-after, meanwhile, trust . . .' All these lead straight into the theological arena at sundry different points: and all these themes have been, and are, the subject of theologians' life-works. The linguistic philosopher may properly congratulate himself on providing new and more acute instruments of analysis, microscopes for the detection of confused thought; but he cannot maintain that he has introduced such novelty or affected such a revolution in philosophical theology, that he can afford to ignore the detailed and scholarly theological studies of just those questions which his own inquiry has shown as fundamental to testing the Christian claims.

Theologians, then, are entirely right to protest when the philosopher light-heartedly discusses theological notions, with no regard to their contexts or their history. They are right to taunt him with professing to be profoundly interested in linguistic *use* and yet making do with the crudest versions of theological concepts, instead of tracing the actual use these concepts receive in a Barth, a Brunner, or a Tillich. If he is to continue the discussion, he will have to do so on theological territory, discussing what actual theologians have written, and exercising his critical acumen on *that*. He will find no lack of scope. If he commits theological howlers through ineptitude, that is a more respectable risk to run than the other risk—the risk of never coming to grips with live theological issues at all.

This book, in a modest way, seeks to make some contribution to that next stage in the discussion, and to do so on theological territory occupied by living writers of some influence. It aims to discover (within a restricted area, necessarily) how certain theologians are tackling those problems of meaning and verification, and how far they are providing an answer to the very real hazards that linguistic philosophy has shown to beset religious language as such.

CHAPTER TWO
COPING WITH PARADOX

———

G OD, says the theologian, acts *in* the world, but does not have his being in the world. He has personal and moral attributes, yet without the features, the voice, the conflicts of choice, the triumphs and failures that go with these in our experience. As outside space and time, he can indeed be no object of experience at all, and yet he is most intimately 'near', the hearer of prayer. He is One God, and yet he is Three. Such paradoxical and near-paradoxical language is the *staple* of accounts of God's nature and is not confined to rhetorical extravaganzas. To Augustine, God was 'good without quality, great without quantity, a creator though he lack nothing, ruling but from no position, eternal yet not in time'.[1]

'Paradox', the sceptical philosopher protests, 'is too optimistic and too solemn a word for all this. It would be more honest to call it a language of *contradiction*, one which can therefore delineate no possible being at all. What sense the right hand puts forward, the left hand whips away again.' It looks as if here the tension between philosopher and theologian is at its maximum.

And yet, 'tension' is not always the right word: for what frustrates and baffles the therapeutically minded philosopher is when the theologian calmly *admits* that all these contradictions, incompatible claims, are there in his writing, just as the philosopher says. He has known they were there and has no intention of abandoning his theology because of their presence. They arise, he explains (and this is often his last word), from the nature of

[1] Augustine, *De Trinitate*.

16

the object of religious language, a being enormously different from any other being whatever—if he may be properly called a being, which is doubtful. Faced with this response, the philosopher easily loses his temper and exclaims: 'Talking with you is impossible. No matter what absurdity, inconsistency, incoherence I locate in your theology, you will (*verbally*, that is) transform it into a new exhibition of the divine "otherness". You don't even recoil when I accuse you of using language without meaning; for, you say, God can use our nonsense as the vehicle of his revelation.' The argument, he feels, has become altogether unreal.

This is the philosopher speaking in excitement and wrath. Sobering, he will reflect that conversation might become possible again, if only one riddle could be answered: When is a contradiction not a *mere* contradiction, but a sublime Paradox, a Mystery? How can we distinguish a viciously muddled confusion of concepts from an excusably stammering attempt to describe what has been glimpsed during some 'raid on the inarticulate', an object too great for our comprehension, but none the less real for that? The philosopher may profitably remind himself that not only in theology but also in science contradictory notions have had to be lived with, for quite long periods. Light, for example, has been studied in our own century by reference to two explanatory models which were thought to be quite incompatible with one another—as wave movements and as particle movements. For years there was no way of knowing whether the dilemma would ever be resolved: it might have had to be endured indefinitely. We can see today that scientists were right to retain both models, despite the conflict between them. Could it not then be the case that the theologian is also right to hold fast to *his* anomalies, even though no conciliatory account is likely to be within our intellectual capacity?

Stop there. What did I mean when I said that the scientist was right to retain the incompatible models? I meant, among other things, that if he had renounced either (in favour of conceptual tidiness and freedom from paradox), he would have lost a hypothesis with immense predictive and explanatory power. To the scientist, that would be about the biggest sacrifice possible. And he is rightly unprepared to make it. Suppose we ask the same question of the theologian: What would be lost if he sacrificed either limb of *his* paradoxes or contradictions? Could he put up a case for retaining them, a case at all parallel to the scientist's?

This looks a promising approach: but we must reckon first with one respect in which the paradoxes in the theologian's account of God do not appear, *prima facie*, to correspond to those of the scientist. Otherwise an important distinction will fail to be made. Sceptics have wanted to say that the contradictions in accounts of God entail that there can *be* no God, just as the contradiction in a 'round square' entails that nothing can *be* a round square. But no one has suggested that because we were forced to use two irreconcilable explanatory models for light—that therefore there could be no such thing as *light*! But why should no one suggest this? Because 'light' is ostensively definable; because, that is to say, you can switch on a lamp in a dark room, and say '*That's* light'. You can draw someone's attention to an actual instance of what the word 'light' is used for. Paradox appears only when we attempt to gather up all we know about light, all the different, experimentally discovered features of its behaviour into one explanatory picture, and we find that two pictures, not one, emerge—a particle-picture and a wave-picture. But where a term receives an ostensive definition, our perplexity at its nature can never rise to such a pitch that we are forced to say, 'It is impossible that this should exist', no matter how unaccountable its behaviour.

One possible way, therefore, in which the theologian might cope with his paradoxes or contradictions is by claiming that in fact the situation of the scientist and his own situation *are* logically parallel, that an ostensive definition of 'God' is obtainable, as well as of 'light'. God cannot be pointed at, brought forward for identification, or indeed made perceptible directly to any of the senses. But he may be encountered as the *Thou* of prayer. I may have a knowledge of him 'by acquaintance', such that (analogous to my glance up at the sun or the lamp) I may raise my 'soul's eye' directly to his presence. And if I can do this, then, although I still have not *resolved* the paradoxes, I can *live* with them with no threat to my faith. In Chapters Three and Four I examine this claim to *I–Thou* encounter with God, particularly as it appears in Buber, Brunner, and Farmer. It is obvious at once that the sort of ostensive definition that is relevant to 'God' must be different in important ways from easy standard cases like the definition of 'light' or 'red' or 'sour'. We shall have to inquire whether these many differences put the definition in jeopardy, whether we can be sure that we are singling out one being without ambiguity, and whether the theologian (like the scientist) takes care to distinguish *what* is ostensively defined from what we may go on to say *about* what has been so defined. In this inquiry we shall conclude that there are numerous ambiguities and uncertainties in the whole procedure, which make it very unlikely that God *can* be ostensively defined, or that we can have such sure 'knowledge by acquaintance' of God as the theologian needs to make his case.

If we assume for the moment that the objections raised in Chapters Three and Four are sound, what alternative ways are there, if any, of coping with the problem? One way suggests itself of avoiding those particular difficulties without abandoning all hope of some sort of ostensive definition.

Since Jesus said, 'He that hath seen me hath seen the Father', the theologian might maintain that ostensive definitions of God consist in pointing at Jesus. 'I and my Father are one': well, then, does this not give us all we need? For if the invisible, intangible God cannot be singled out for ostensive definition, God incarnate *may* be so singled out. In fact it might be held that the point of the incarnation was just that this should happen. Thus a 'Christocentric' theology can be built up, a theology that seeks to construe all statements about God as, in the end, statements about Jesus. Some features of this theological approach, a very influential one at the present time, are considered in Chapter Five. To anticipate once again: I shall argue that it is outstandingly successful in according to the incarnation that centrality in Christian thought which it merits, but in so doing it raises serious new problems of its own. The gravest of these appear when one asks about the relation between Jesus and God the Father. This relation certainly cannot be identity, despite the texts quoted above; for Jesus came from God, prayed to him, asked why he had forsaken him, and went back to God. This approach does not reckon adequately with the great logical gulf between talk about the man Jesus and talk about the *transcendent* deity. We start out hoping to be able to do for 'God' what pointing will do for 'light', and to do this by pointing at Jesus instead. But to analyse this procedure in some detail shows it to be disappointingly rich in the production of new paradoxes of its own.

Let us suppose now that ostensive definition, both direct and indirect, fails. We are now in the position of a scientist who not only had contradictory explanatory models of something or other, but was *also* unable to say, 'Look; there is an instance of what I am talking about.' It is tempting to capitulate here and imagine that the only option left would be to classify 'God' with 'round square', taking both as notions that are internally contradictory in a vicious way, and which therefore cannot refer to any possible existent. But there is a yet unconsidered possibility: and again the scientist may provide us with an analogy. *Suppose* that in order to make sense of certain experimental data a scientist posits a 'new' sub-atomic particle 'P'. Attributing certain properties to P helps with the framing of useful hypotheses which he otherwise could not frame. But the more he investigates P, the more conceptual difficulties he finds in mapping its total behaviour. He cannot describe P without using paradoxical language. More annoying still, because P is sub-atomic, he cannot get hold of an *instance* of it, so as to exhibit its reality to himself and his colleagues. The most he can do is to record the *probability* of there being a P in such and such a position at such and such a time. His laws about the behaviour of *P*s are *statistical* laws, not laws accurately governing the behaviour of individual *P*s in accurately described circumstances. We may assume that in such a situation we should be forced to say that *P* cannot be ostensively defined.[1] But need the scientist abandon the concept of *P* because of that? Not at all. He would be still justified in positing *P* because of its value in framing hypotheses, in making sense of phenomena that without it would remain unpredictable, or unrelated to better understood phenomena. If he is challenged as to why he believes there are *P*s, when he can neither single them out nor speak of them without paradox, he is entitled to appeal to all those theoretical and practical advantages which are his only through his 'belief in' *P*s.

Now the theologian. If ostensive definition fails him, could he not say exactly the same? 'If we *were* to abandon all talk of "God" (paradox-ridden though it is), we should immediately cease to be able to make sense of many things which that concept *does* make sense of. Far more sensible, then, to hold on to the paradoxes than to jettison the religious language.' This would imply that certain experiences (say of beauty or of absolute moral demands), or certain events in history, can be far better understood if brought into relation with the idea of God, or maybe not understood at all until they *are* brought into relation with it. Chapters Six and Seven discuss claims of this kind regarding historical events; in particular the critical events recorded in the New Testament. Chapter Eight asks: How much more sense, if any, does belief in God make of *moral* ideas? Or, putting it the other way round, is moral seriousness equally possible to believer and sceptic, or possible only to the believer? These three chapters are thus concerned with God as the alleged explanation of limited sets of events or experiences of particular types. In Chapters Nine and Ten I look at some arguments that try to show that *nothing whatever* can be explained without invoking God. As far

---

[1] It may be that in fact scientists are *not* confronted with this situation in regard to any actual particle. Our illustration would not be affected. It is sufficient if the situation is conceivable: which it is.

as these arguments go, our experiences and the actual course of events might have been radically different from what they are and were, without impairing the clearest and greatest testimony to God's existence, namely the existence of a universe that requires him as its author and sustainer.

Again our conclusions are reluctantly negative. God *may* be the explanation demanded by some set of events or by the sum of events: but the groups of arguments discussed here do not seem to me to establish their case. If ostensive definition and explanatory hypothesis both fail as attempts to justify retaining the logically tortured language of religion, it is very hard to see what justification is left.

The believer may say that he is willing to dispense with the whole idea of justification, and to continue believing nevertheless. He may simply declare that, for him, to be confronted with the Jesus of the New Testament is to be compelled to worship, and to be compelled to accept Jesus' uniquely authoritative words about himself and about God. Verification, explanation are religiously irrelevant (and irreverent) ideas. One cannot be reasoned into belief, nor have one's belief rationally justified; one can only be converted, make the leap of faith. This position cannot be refuted, since no reasoned objection can reach to its nerve—a nerve avowedly non-rational. It provides the first topic of the final chapter.

The second topic is this. Little serious thought is given usually to the religiously minded person who *does* suspect a total failure in theology, who finds (unlike the bold believer referred to in the last paragraph) that he cannot without losing his intellectual integrity retain any sort of Christian orthodoxy, and to whom yet the loss of all belief is a bewildering prospect. How far, we shall ask, can something like a religious orientation of life be retained— even in a 'dark night of the intellect'? The fear that *nothing* of this can be kept constantly drives people to cling desperately and doubtingly to discredited arguments for belief, which for them can be no more than rationalizations of a *will* to believe, a will not to lose all sense that life has a 'meaning' nor to have to discard those imaginative sources of moral enrichment which the myths, parables, symbols, stories of the Bible had furnished abundantly in a time of belief. The knowledge that there may be 'prepared positions' to which to withdraw if orthodox faith breaks down— that life can still have meaning and the parables and symbols still be effective—can give a person a measure of reassurance, which enables him to continue the theological debate with a greater calm of mind than if he felt continually on a precipice-edge.

No doubt, those who believe that the precipice-edge is the very best place to keep a man while the Gospel is preached to him (or *at* him) will protest at this bid to relieve his anguish. Philosophy, it will be said, may require the tranquillity of the study, but not so the theology of crisis and commitment. But then, one of the things that these studies hope to show is that even *those* kinds of theology speak a language that can be coherent or *in*-coherent, sensible or nonsensical. They can manage skilfully their points of contact with ordinary language; or muddle these in a murk of ambiguity. All these possibilities interest the philosopher of religion; as indeed they ought to interest the theologian himself. If they have *not* interested him enough recently, one might infer with fair confidence that the precipice, although a good place from which to take leaps, has not proved so congenial to clear thinking.

CHAPTER THREE

'ENCOUNTERS' (1)

———

I

THEOLOGIANS who believe that it is possible to encounter God directly, and so to offer, as we have been saying, some kind of ostensive definition of him, have recently been arguing along the following lines.

If God were an object like a hidden vein of gold or a heavenly body, too small or too remote for the telescope, then observation and argument, verifying procedures and speculation might be adequate for searching him out. But if he is no object, if instead he is a *person*, the whole situation is changed, and quite another approach to him is demanded. We approach *things* in detachment, confident that they will passively suffer our scrutiny, that our discoveries about them can be corroborated by others. Persons, on the other hand, reveal themselves fully only if we renounce our detachment and enter into reciprocal relations with them. The impact a person makes upon me may be unique to the point of being incommunicable to anyone else. The abstractness of speculation or systems of ideas is quite hostile to the immediacy and concreteness of personal encounters. Even if apologists successfully demonstrated by argument that God exists, such speculation could lead only to a 'God of the philosophers', to an impersonal, remote First Principle. The living God, the God of Abraham, can be authentically known only to the man who addresses him as *Thou*, who finds him in the unique directness of personal contact.

Of course, a human being is not distinctively personal in all circumstances or forever. He weighs so many stones, occupies so many cubic feet; he stumbles or sits on his hat when wishing to be most thoroughly poised and personal. He also dies. God, however, never becomes an *It*, an object: he is eternally a *Thou* only. There is no detecting *his* presence by bumps on the stair or even a whispered word or the glimpse of a face. We cannot, with *him*, point or glance in this or that direction, and say, 'There, he is coming now.' We have only that felt sense of personal meeting, a sense of addressing and being addressed. He leaves no marks of his presence such that we might say—'This proves he is with us.' There is nothing for the camera or the tape-recorder. For all these and the like evidences involve the degrading of God from being a pure *Thou* to an *It*, passively at our disposal.

We should therefore be advised to cease demanding the impossible, that the existence of God should be verifiable like the presence of a chair or a table, or leave traces like a burglar who drops his jemmy. We have no right to expect the ostensive definition of 'God' to be in every respect parallel to that of 'light' (in our original example). The one appropriate procedure is to entrust ourselves in prayer to the being who is properly only talked *to*, not theorized *about*. There need be no fear of rendering our faith irrational or unsupported through this exchange. Instead of depending on uncertain chains of reasoning, we should depend on a self-authenticating direct awareness of God; a knowledge by acquaintance, from which all fallible inference-steps are absent. If the philosopher declares himself unhappy about this exchange, and suspects that it disguises a retreat to a pietistic concern with feelings and attitudes only, then he can be accused of shirking the venture of faith, a venture not of swallowing hard doctrine, but of self-commitment to the divine *Thou*, a commitment without which God's being remains veiled from us. Or if he tries but fails to have any sense of encounter with God, we must conclude that he is insensitive to the divine *Thou*, much as a colour-blind man is insensitive to certain colour-distinctions or a tone-deaf man to musical intervals. Only, *this* insensitivity, unlike the others, may be ultimately rooted in sin.

A very considerable number of non-Roman Catholic theologians writing today endorse these views or similar ones. Divergences would of course appear as soon as we asked questions about exactly *how* the divine–human encounter takes place, the role of symbol and sacrament in meeting God, and the extent to which God is known 'through' Christ. In this and the following chapter, however, we shall be much more concerned with what unites these theologians than with what sunders them. And no single writer has contributed more influentially to the statement of those views than has Martin Buber, to whose work we shall first turn.

Buber's analysis of personal relations, given classical expression in his short but difficult book *I and Thou*, has provided not only the central thesis—that knowledge of God is irreducibly personal, but also much of the vocabulary, the distinctions, the either/or's, which the discussion of that thesis continues to employ. To Buber, the two 'primary words' *I–Thou* and *I–It*, describe two fundamentally different, mutually exclusive forms of our relation to our world. A being is an *It* to us when we study it with a view to manipulating it, mastering it, classifying it, comparing it with other things. Human beings also are *It*s (or what comes to the same thing, *He*s and *She*s) when regarded in these ways, treated as objects of our curiosity, sources of useful information, or exploitable means to our pleasure. In these cases we are not, in Buber's language, properly in relation with persons *as* persons: their personal being eludes us entirely. *I–It* relations must inevitably dominate many aspects of our living; but the man or woman who knows only *I–It* and is a stranger to *I–Thou* is excluded both from freedom and from 'real life'.

Since the *I–It* relation can span both things *and* people, so too can the *I–Thou* relation. A natural object, say a mountain, can cease to be seen as an obstacle to the road-builder or as the stance for a fine view or a likely haunt for the eagle, and become for me a *Thou* in Buber's sense, something with which I am directly related, aware of its individuality, its uniqueness. I am not in this case concerned with this or that *aspect* of it, but I simply contemplate it as it is in itself, 'bodied over against me'.[1] There is here even a faint sense of reciprocity. The mountain or lake or tree 'has to do with me, as I with it—only in a different way . . . Relation is mutual'.[2]

With human beings naturally, the reciprocity is much more explicit. To know a person is not merely to know that his eyes are grey, his hair brown, his patience inexhaustible. It is not to know any list of characteristics, however long a list. If what we are out to do is take note of characteristics, we are still in the relation of *I–It*, the spectator *vis-à-vis* the *object* of his scrutiny. In sharp contrast,

> I do not experience the man to whom I say *Thou*. But I take my stand in relation to him, in the sanctity of the primary word. . . . in the act of experience *Thou* is far away.
> All real living is meeting.[3]

All human *I–Thou* encounters pave the way for the encounter with the eternal *Thou*. Conviction of God's existence is not the result of any process of argument, for God is 'the Being that is directly, most nearly, and lastingly, over against us, that may properly only be addressed, not expressed'.[4] The moment a person begins to make an inventory of the features of the person who has been *Thou* to him, that person becomes *It* instead. But when someone detaches himself from the *divine* encounter and tries to give *it* objectivity by listing whatever half-glimpsed features he can recall of *that* meeting, he finds the original situation is being far *more* radically warped in the very describing of it. He sets out to speak of God, but finds he has spoken of something else, or discovers with dismay that he has nothing to speak of at all. But

[1] Martin Buber, *I and Thou* (Edinburgh: T. & T. Clark, 1937), p. 8.
[2] *Ibid., loc. cit.*   [3] *Ibid.*, pp. 9, 11.   [4] *Ibid.*, pp. 80 ff.

from the poverty of our descriptions nothing follows about the fact of the encounter itself. Indeed, the *I–Thou* relation is consummated, becomes fully pure, only in the encounter with God as 'absolute person'.

All this is the merest paraphrase of Buber's central teaching. Further aspects of it will emerge during the comments and criticisms I am going on to make. But first it may be helpful to substantiate the claim that the Jewish thinker, Buber, has profoundly influenced many of the best-known *Christian* theologians. The new emphasis on *meeting* rather than thinking *about* is nowhere clearer than in Emil Brunner's *The Divine–Human Encounter*. Brunner aims to return to 'Reformation principles' by rejecting both what he calls 'objectivist' *and* 'subjectivist' standpoints with regard to our knowledge of God. Knowing God, Brunner believes, is not receiving revealed information about him (the objective view): but it is no truer to say that God is known through the devout feelings of worshippers (the subjective option). Denying both alternatives, Brunner says he is known only through encountering him in faith. This is not the communicating of information, but an 'event . . . an act'. Faith is no simple 'believing *that*' such and such is the case, but is 'the single "answering" acceptance of the Word of God'. Knowing God is not analogous to making a scientific discovery, but is much more clearly analogous to our encounters with human beings.[1]

Professor H. H. Farmer in *The World and God* follows Buber in making the strongest contrast between knowledge of *It*s and knowledge of *Thou*s. He holds that personal awareness has an immediacy or directness, which guarantees its distinctiveness. It is perceived within a 'direct responsive relationship'. *God* as personal is perceived most clearly in the pressure upon us of unconditional values, which can be interpreted most reasonably as the impact of his will. The experience of divine encounter 'in the nature of the case must be self-authenticating and able to

[1] Emil Brunner, *The Divine–Human Encounter* (London: S.C.M., 1944), pp. 15, 20, 28, 34, 49, 59.

shine in its own light, independently of the abstract reflections of philosophy . . .'[1]

Karl Barth is equally sure that God does not present himself to us as an object for verification. God is the 'Subject that remains indissolubly Subject'. He sees, however, as some theologians seem (oddly) to forget, that a person who loves someone may well choose to put himself in some sense 'at the disposal' of the other. To remain hidden and elusive would tend to thwart rather than further their love. In the Incarnation God does exactly this: puts himself at man's disposal; permits man to touch and handle, even to kill. But Barth's position is a complex one. He denies that through successful historical research, say, belief could be *forced* on someone. For knowledge of Christ also must remain *personal* knowledge. He cannot be known like an object at the mercy of the researcher, but only in encounter.

In numerous Christian theologies (including the ones just mentioned) Buber's views are not simply reproduced, but are often considerably transformed. Perhaps the most frequent change is the intensifying of Buber's already dramatic contrast between the standpoints of *I–Thou* and *I–It*. Sin comes to be regarded as a kind of imprisonment in the world of *I–It*; that is to say, an inability to respond as a person to others. But our immediate purpose is not greatly complicated by variations on the main *I–Thou* theme: for that purpose is to appraise critically the whole attempt to argue for an immediate, self-authenticating encounter with God.

2

The main features of this approach can only be welcomed by the philosopher of religion. If the methods of verification that philosophers bring to religious statements are suitable for confirming the existence of *objects*, and if God is 'irreducibly *Subject*',

[1] H. H. Farmer, *The World and God* (London: Nisbet, 1935), pp. 9, 14, 18, 23 ff., 158, 162.

irreducibly *personal*, the application of these methods will quite misleadingly (perhaps falsely) proclaim that God does not exist. This warning is salutary, not only to the traditional 'rational theologian' with his speculative arguments for God's existence, but equally to the linguistic philosopher whose 'hangover' from positivism tempts him to think of verification as *par excellence* the confirmation of scientific hypotheses.

The religious person is always on edge, and rightly so, lest talk *about* God should for some reflective people replace prayer and self-committal *to* God, lest these people should exchange the all-important encounter with God for the (far less important) entertaining of more or less adequate ideas about him. The theology of *I* and *Thou* certainly ensures that the language of prayer is given priority over the language of reflection.

Yet we have to ask if the strongest claims of this theology are justified: if knowledge of God as personal can be entirely self-authenticating, or whether there is room here for (and even likelihood of) error and illusion. Can we accept that sharp division —either arguments for God *or* personal encounter; nothing in between? Are there no checking-procedures relevant to the encounter of person with person? Or does all 'checking' necessarily degrade persons to the status of things? If the vital analogy here is that between meeting people and meeting God, have the theologians established this analogy firmly enough to bear the weighty superstructure that they have reared upon it?

It is most unlikely that any conclusive argument could be brought against someone's claim to have met God in personal encounter. The great problem, we shall see, is to fathom how far this claim is in fact a bare record of the *immediate* encounter, as it purports to be, and how far that experience has been interpreted (and perhaps *mis*interpreted) by the subject in his very attempt to 'make sense' of it. Whom or what was he aware of directly meeting—'the God of our Lord Jesus Christ', God as 'Creator of heaven and earth', a Supernatural being, or a 'numinous', awful Presence? The question, which of these or other possible answers he will give, is of the first importance; for if the original direct encounter was with a being known in the last-mentioned way—as a holy and dreadful Presence—then one could *not* claim to have been aware, directly and immediately, of (say) God as Father of Jesus Christ. The judgement, 'I encountered the God revealed uniquely in the New Testament' would be an indirect, not a direct judgement. It would depend on inferences that could not themselves claim 'self-authentication'. We shall also have to consider the objection that such certainty as the Christian claims for his encounters with God can be had only by 'subjective' or 'psychological' statements: statements *not* to the effect that such and such exists or is the case, but that I have such and such sensations and feelings, and no more. And from statements as cautious as those one may *not* infer any equally certain statements about the world, about things or persons other than the speaker.

In the encounter between man and God, Brunner says:

> An exchange takes place . . . which is wholly without analogy in the sphere of thinking. The sole analogy is in the encounter between human beings, the meeting of person with person.

Human encounters, however, are unstable and impure. They alternate between genuine *I–Thou* relations and degraded *I–It* relations. But they can still serve as a guide to what *pure I–Thou* encounter with God must be.

> When I stand opposite to God, I am face to face with him who unconditionally is no 'something', who in the unconditional sense is pure 'Thou'.[1]

That is to say, human encounters provide the classical analogy with divine–human encounters. We can move, in thought, away from the imperfections of our *human*-encounter examples towards an idea of the perfection of the meeting with God. This we

[1] *The Divine–Human Encounter*, pp. 59 f.

do by thinking away all that remains of *I–It*, all vacillating between experiencing the other as personal and as object, until there remains nothing at all of object-knowledge, only pure encounter with a *Thou*.

The use of the words 'pure' and 'mixed' or 'impure' of encounters implies that we could construct a scale of relative purity (within our experience of human meetings) and then project it to its limiting, extreme case in the encounter with God. If we cannot give meaning to this movement of thought, then we shall not be able to understand exactly what 'pure' and 'impure' signify here. But that breakdown in meaning would have serious consequences. We should not know what elements in the analogy direct us towards understanding the encounter with God, and what elements do not. We want above all to know whether the rails of analogy on which Brunner sets us run smoothly in the direction he points. And it is exactly this that begins to look uncertain. Consider three situations:

(*a*) Suppose I am talking to someone, and suddenly notice that he is looking at me in an odd and disquieting way. What, I ask myself, is he up to? I decide he is simply and literally looking *at* me, observing carefully my hand and arm movements, taking note of what I do with my eyes, how I modulate my voice. I feel as if I were in a shop-window on show, not engaged in what is meant to be mutual conversation.

This situation would pass as radically 'impure'. I am being treated as an *It*. (Perhaps the other man is studying me in order to be able to imitate me at a party.)

(*b*) I have known Tom for a short time only, but our relations are rapidly becoming friendly and relaxed. He sits opposite me now, and he watches my hand, arm, and eyes, listens to my voice. But I should want to say that he does not use these as objects of curiosity, but uses them in order to enter into living relation with me. In this case, the impurity is much lessened.

(c) John is my fast and long-established friend. He is walk-ing with me, and it is half-dark. We do not mind not being able to see hands, arms, eyes very clearly. There are long pauses between our remarks. But the silences are not wastes of time or embarrassing failures in *rapport*. We are still nearer Brunner's 'purity'.

In view of these illustrations, does it not look as if there *is* a scale here of, first, diminishing concern with human beings as objects; and, second, increasing purity of *I–Thou* relationship? Why should this *not* be projectible quite meaningfully and help-fully to its limit in man's meeting with God, alone 'purely per-sonal'? It is tempting to say 'Why not indeed?': but we should be most incautious, if we did. Is it true that in moving from (a) to (c) the physical events (hands, eyes, voice, in movement and sound) have become progressively less essential; or have they re-mained quite essential in each case, although approached, used, attended to, in different ways, or checked up on less and less fre-quently because of the increasing intimacy of the people con-cerned? If the second alternative were correct, then purification would *not* have been shown to run parallel to dwindling reliance on 'knowing facts *about*' the other man, and the movement of thought which the analogy demands would not manage even to start.

Before we examine this possibility, we have to distinguish three different questions, which often become woefully confused. They refer to three different situations in which verification-problems may arise quite naturally in human relations.

(i) We may ask, 'Is there someone in the room, or is that a heap of clothes, a bolster in the bed, the shadow of a suitcase?' This sort of question may be answered without any need to enter into *I–Thou* relations with the person, if person there be. We turn up the light, pull back the bedclothes, look in the corner, and so on.

(ii) We may ask, 'Is James really unhappy, or does he show all the signs of misery, while being inwardly light of heart?' This is a problem about our knowledge of other people's minds. In practice, we may have to become a close friend of James before we can be sure in all circumstances, if *ever* we can be sure. But still we are dealing with what Buber would insist was an *I–It* relation; concerned with the discovery of facts about a person, facts that we can express in general terms—he really is sad, he really is a practical joker, he really is insane. As in the other case, we are quite dependent on the evidence of our senses, or on what James does, says, or betrays of his state of mind.

(iii) We may ask, 'How can I describe my personal relations with John, the peculiar impact his personality makes on me?' Any list, however extended, of his characteristics allows the all-important thing, the uniqueness, to slip through unexpressed. To do justice to it, I should have to add an account of all I have done with John, places visited together, the thousand chats and discussions, exchanges of letters: for all these more or less determine the *timbre* of our relationship. But how could anyone else sense the exact flavour these give it for me? General terms here seem to break down; and, significantly, they fail us just when a relationship appears most definitely to become *I–Thou*.

Yet notice that when we are in an *I–Thou* situation, talking with John, say, by firelight, we may quite easily make mistakes on each of the three levels we have just spoken of.

(i) I may speak to John, 'sensing' his presence with me, although unknown to me John may have quietly slipped out of the room, thinking that I had fallen asleep.

(ii) I may some day mistakenly interpret John's excitement as indicating a piece of good fortune; whereas it really is a sign of nervous tension over some personal crisis that I have not heard about.

(iii) Something John tells me one day about himself, or something I see him do, convinces me that I have never really known his 'centre' or his true personality. The kaleidoscope is suddenly re-shuffled, a quite *new* 'uniqueness' is given to my relation with him. The impression I had formerly had of his personality was a highly particular one, concrete and impossible to generalize about (like all good *I–Thou* instances)—yet in some way it was fraught with illusion. What I believed was the *Thou* over against me, directly apprehended, has proved to have been my (false) inter-pretation of, or construction out of, what John seemed to me to be. I realize with a jolt what a crucial role is played by knowledge *about* John even in my *I* and *Thou* relation with him. He is now quite different to me; and it was the glimpse of an act or hearing a word that has brought about the change.

The fact that we can make occasional mistakes about encounters with human beings (as in these examples) would not necessarily make nonsense of the scale of 'purity'. What *does* upset it is a fact brought out by the same examples—namely, the continuing importance of 'knowledge about' or 'knowledge *that*' in even the most intimate relationships. Only the unexpected disappointment brings home to us that although we rarely or never *list* the charac-teristics our friend displays, we presuppose them nevertheless during every moment of our relationship. My ease of mind during John's silences is inductively justified by my memory of the count-less times he has ended such a silence with words that showed he had been meditating on someting I had said to him, and not with a yawn of boredom and a glance at the clock. The longer one has known somebody, and the more experience one has gathered of him, the longer the gaps that one can allow between checking in various ways upon his reaction to what is being said and done. In *this* sense one is not so dependent on information *about* him, on facts about what he is *like*, as in less intimate relationships. But again, this is so only because we assume consistency in our friend's personality. Whereas, the actual forms that his consistent behaviour takes we have had to learn by watching, asking, and listening.

On the occasions when I sit opposite a friend and observe his gestures and expression, I am neither looking *at* these as at so many objects, nor in the belief that his entire personal being consists in such overt actions (behaviourism), nor am I looking 'through' these to the *hidden* personality, as I might look through the glass of a window, concerned only with the view beyond. His behaviour is not being taken as a 'window' into his immaterial, ghostly 'mind'. I admit that his inner life, like mine, is more than gestures, speech, smiles; but I doubt if we know what we are saying when we declare that personality and knowledge of personality are possible without these; I doubt if anything recognizably personal can be left over, once we have mentally stripped all such behaviour away.

I think I am saying more than that all human *I–Thou* encounters remain full of 'impurities' through their dependence on 'knowledge about'. The peculiar difficulty is to know how even theoretically the situation could be improved. If we seriously try to conceive circumstances in which we might claim to have done away with all behavioural checks in communing with someone, we will find either that we have in a peculiar way failed to maintain the separate identities of the two people concerned, or that we have no means of knowing whether we are in *rapport* with someone or not, which do not ultimately rely upon the behavioural checks themselves.[1] For consider the possibilities.

I might imagine that the ideal here would be a state where I did not have to see John flush, hear him slam doors, and shout, to know that he was angry: but simply knew it as John knows it himself. I should feel the ascent of blood to the head, the kinæsthetic feelings that go with cry-uttering and door-slamming, the

---

[1] Readers of John Wisdom's *Other Minds* (Oxford: Blackwell, 1952) will recognize my occasional borrowings from the illustrations in that book in the present chapter. They will also need no telling that I am not attempting to reproduce Wisdom's own argument faithfully.

tension and temptation to lose control. But how could this be distinguished from temporarily *becoming John*? This would be not to *encounter* some other personality, but to *assume* another personality. Or, if that sounds too fantastic, one could describe the situation in quite another way: by saying that instead of en-countering an angry John (which was my original aim), I now merely become angry myself—a very different thing.

Alternatively, I might not reproduce John's sensations, but in-stead (by telepathy) see a red circle in the air when John was angry, a blue cross when he felt happy, and so on. But how could I ever know that this was a dependable 'code'? Only by checking up systematically with John himself (speaking to him, listening to him, watching him), and finding if my circles and crosses did correspond with his angers and delights. Unless I was prepared to trust such checks, i.e. to rely on the *normal* ways of discovering other people's states of mind, I would have no grounds at all for saying that my mental diagrams gave me knowledge of his mind.

Notice too that these fantasies have been operating only at what we have called level (ii)—where the question is an *I–It* question about what someone is thinking or feeling. If we ask what reciprocal, truly personal relations would be like when 'purified' to the point where no 'knowledge about' or 'memory that' or behavioural check was involved, the difficulties are enor-mously magnified.

In face of these reflections, the theologian might well decide that the analogy between meeting human beings and meeting God is too weak to carry any apologetic weight. But, rather than capitulate, he may choose to make a last-ditch stand. He could make it by staking all on that sense of utter uniqueness that is involved in all genuine *I–Thou* relations. If in fact all description using general terms fails to capture that uniqueness, surely the pith of personal-encounter experiences cannot be certain com-plexes of memories and present sensations: surely, that is, it is *possible* for the *I–Thou* situation to survive the pruning away of all these impurities?

This might be plausible, if it were true that individuality and uniqueness *cannot* depend on a complex interrelation of general factors. But we are in a position only to say that it often is hard to see what all the factors are and how their interrelating could produce precisely the effect it *does* produce. This is a recurrent and familiar situation in art or literary criticism. At first sight it is simply inexplicable how, say, a simple-looking stanza makes its wholly individual impact on the reader. It seems incredible that it could be only a matter of the interrelation of the senses and sounds of the everyday words that compose it. Thorough examination may begin to show just *how* the various suggestions, associations, near and remote, of these ingredients fuse together; and even though the analysis failed to account *completely* for the effect of the stanza, it might dispel our initial incredulity. Yes, we say, the effect is due to a subtle combination of meanings, overlaying one another, intensifying, qualifying one another. And so with the impact of one human being on another. Those factors mentioned earlier—the strata of memories of all the meetings, all the shared experiences—all far too numerous and complex to analyse exhaustively—may well fuse in a closely parallel way, and generate a similar sense of utter individuality. But to ask for the strikingness of that stanza without the words, to expect that there could be impact of personality without memories and sensations, would be like demanding the grin of the Cheshire cat without the cat itself.

To ask someone to think analogically is to ask him (*a*) to imagine some familiar item of experience, which is to afford a clue to the nature of what is unknown; and (*b*) to give him directions how to *modify* this item of experience so as to increase its resemblance to the unknown and diminish its inadequacy. For example, I may give a child some idea of the solar system by constructing an arrangement of table-lamps and tennis-balls; directing him to imagine the originals as so many thousand times larger than the models, and different in other, specified ways. But if we are not able to give clear indication of how to modify the familiar, no analogical thinking is possible. It is of no avail to insist nonetheless that there *is* an analogy somewhere, though we cannot say quite where. Now, we have been examining the claimed analogy between meeting human beings and meeting God as pure person. We have seen that although different sorts of human relationship make different sorts of use of bodily features, sounds, and appearances, there is still nothing to suggest that these become progressively less and less necessary as the relationship becomes purer: nothing therefore to imply that there is a purest of all relationships, in which they are quite superfluous. We have *not* been given the clear directions for modifying the familiar that we must have for safe analogical thinking. This analogy is like a car that stalls at the very start of a race.

3

All the same, there might be other ways of speaking about personal encounter with God that are immune to these criticisms. We might consider, for example, the presentation of this theme in the work of H. H. Farmer.

Farmer's argument begins, promisingly enough, with the statement that, although personal knowledge of people is in some sense direct or immediate, it is by no means independent of 'bodily manifestations'. He denies that

the immediate awareness of personality in another is necessarily given through any and every impression his body may make upon us: it is only when those impressions are part of a certain direct, responsive relationship . . . that through them the dimension of the personal is immediately perceived. . . .[1]

Nothing said in this chapter conflicts with these claims. We should especially endorse the distinction between immediacy and

[1] *The World and God*, p. 18.

independence. Our last few paragraphs have aimed precisely at heightening this contrast. Nevertheless, it is doubtful whether Farmer holds on to his own insight consistently. He proceeds to ask what sort of relation is most distinctively personal, and answers—the relationship of trust. Central to this is 'an awareness of the other's will as standing over against our own in a certain polarity or tension'.[1] Two pages further on this becomes: 'This might be said to be what personality supremely is, namely that type of conscious being who is capable of entering into such a mutual relationship of trust.' And then, later in the same work, he speaks of 'that ultimate polarity of wills which *is* personal relationship'.[2] From here there is an easy transition to Farmer's account of personal knowledge of God. 'Will' is the obvious crucial common factor between human and divine encounter-experiences.

> The religious man is aware of a certain peculiar type of resistance being set up within the sphere of his values and preferences: the resistance, namely, of absolute, sacred, unconditional values. . . . it is in and through the accent of unconditionality that the awareness of meeting another's will in and through such values is given . . . Whose will is it, then, that is met in such unconditional value-resistance? To the religious mind it is the will of God . . . And 'will' means 'person'.[3]

Encounter with God, once more, is self-authenticating, 'known only through direct perception not describable in other terms'.[4]

My anxiety about this is that the transition from human to divine encounters (whether or not valid) has been made to look deceptively smooth. We learn the use of the word 'will' by being shown people persisting in difficult tasks, ignoring distractions, grunting and perspiring with effort, and so on. We remember

---

[1] *The World and God*, p. 19.   [2] *Ibid.*, p. 162; italics mine.
[3] *Ibid.*, pp. 23 f.
[4] *Towards Belief in God* (London: S.C.M., 1942), Part I, p. 41.

ourselves clearing our desk of holiday snapshots, keeping our pen moving though the wrist ached, muttering to ourselves, 'However long it takes me, I'll finish it tonight.' What is very doubtful indeed is whether anyone could conceivably be in a position to say, 'I am sure X is "willing", but this is not revealed through his uttering a command or by signs of tension on his face or hands, or by other resolute behaviour. Nor did he predict or promise or otherwise give me reason to believe that he would exercise his will at this hour of the day.' The point at stake here is not that Farmer is necessarily wrong when he stresses the importance of will in personal relations. The misleading move is in the statement, 'will means person'. This is true (and trivial) if it means 'once you are entitled to claim contact with someone's will, you are entitled to claim contact with that person'. For instance, I have heard the resolute commands, seen the clenching of fists, noted the absence of wavering. This is indeed the Sergeant-major, and no wraith. But it by no means follows that if I have an experience that I want to call 'experiencing a will' (a sense as of a will over against me), I am entitled to say, 'I am therefore in contact with a person (although the usual manifestations are lacking).'

This is not to deny that we do have experiences that tempt us very strongly to say, 'Another's will is backing up my own will'; 'I keep hearing something like a command inside me, and it is not I who utter it.' The notion of 'will-resistance' or 'will-reinforcement', where no manifestations occur, does seem intelligible. For example: (*a*) Someone may feel sustained while on active service by the knowledge than an intimate friend is backing up his morale with his or her own will. Unfortunately, the sense of the soldier that this is so cannot be relied upon as an argument to the existence and continued 'willing' of the friend. Unknown to the soldier, the friend may have died, the sweetheart may have become unfaithful. There is a fairy-tale which Louis MacNeice retold in his play *The Dark Tower*, in which the hero is given a ring that infallibly tells by its changes of colour whether or not the hero's mother still wishes him to endure in his pilgrimage. But in real life the 'sense of encounter with a will' has no such infallibility.

Or again (*b*) there is the neurotic who is kept from action that he knows is morally harmless by his sense of a will in opposition to his own, a will whose behests he must obey at any cost. And yet the will is *nobody's* will, for all its power. It is not his father's will; for his father is all affection and sympathy. It is not his father as he was when the neurotic was a child (although this is nearer the truth): but it is that child's distorted and warped impression of his father—the will, that is, of someone who does not exist now and never has existed. In neither instance (*a*) or (*b*) can a safe inference be drawn from 'sense of will here' to 'therefore I am in personal contact with someone over against me'.

'In neither of *these* cases,' Farmer might agree, 'but my case is different. For it is in the unique experience of recognizing absolute values that I say our awareness of God as personal will is given.' Quite: we shall have to examine that particular claim on its own merits.

The essential contrast on which it depends is that between asserting a 'conditional' and asserting an 'unconditional' value-judgement. Farmer wants to say that the unconditional judgements, those which have priority over all rivals, can be satisfactorily accounted for only by seeing in them the will of God. It is only because God wills these policies of conduct that they can come to have absolute and sacred binding authority over me. 'As Heim has said, man cannot lay an unconditional on his own will by his own will.' [1]

It can be argued, however, that this position contains an important inconsistency. If we are going to say that a moral principle loses all its 'ifs' and 'buts' by being shown to be willed by God, then we must be assuming as an indispensable premiss that God's will is itself unconditionally good—otherwise the fact that he backed up some moral judgement of ours would do

[1] *The World and God*, pp. 23 f.

nothing to settle the question of its absoluteness or even its rightness.

Now here is a judgement to the effect that something is unconditionally, absolutely good, namely God's will. It is (necessarily) we ourselves who are making this judgement. But on Farmer's view absoluteness is given only by adding to a judgement about morals the further judgement that 'this is willed by God'. But when it is that very will which is being evaluated, judged to be unconditionally good (as it has to be for Farmer's approach to succeed), then obviously *that* judgement cannot be given *its* authority in the same way as the other judgements. Or else we should be saying that our trust in the goodness of God's will is given absoluteness by the fact that what he wills he wills! We are instead forced to conclude that human beings are able to make *of themselves* at least one very bold unconditional value-judgement, the judgement that God's will is unconditionally good. Without this judgement we have no way of knowing whether or not coincidence with God's will gives absoluteness (or anything else) to moral judgements we make. But if we can make this one judgement, it can no longer be said that the sense of unconditional obligation is understandable only as encounter with God's will.[1]

Farmer, however, admits that 'it is not possible to exclude logically all other possible causes of the unconditionality of the moral imperative'. He is not offering a demonstrative proof of God's existence, but showing only that the theistic interpretation of moral experience is the most reasonable one. We recollect that *instead* of demonstrative proof Farmer speaks of our self-authenticating encounter with a personal God, met and recognized in the impact of the divine will, the 'bearer' of absolute values, and in the assurance of what he calls 'final succour'. But if it is by no means sure that the assertion of unconditional values does require the idea of some divine bearer, and moreover if we must be able to

[1] Discussion of related issues on moral judgement and the divine will can also be found in Chapter Eight, below.

make unconditional judgements which are logically *unable* to have this support (like the judgement that God's will confers absolute bindingness), then can it possibly be held that the sense of encounter with God is in any real sense 'self-authenticating'? It would be self-authenticating only if the Farmer account of absolute value had turned out to be demonstrably and unchallengeably adequate. But it has to be judged, for logical reasons, an incomplete and *in*adequate account. Yet it is in *that* way that we should have to interpret experiences of absolute moral demand in order to be compelled to take them as experiences of meeting God.

It is no help to say with Farmer that Christian experience of God '. . . in the nature of the case *must* be self-authenticating and able to shine by its own light independently of the abstract reflections of philosophy, for if it were not, it could hardly be a living experience of God as personal'.[1]

That phrase 'in the nature of the case' is marvellously question-begging. For we are supremely concerned to discover what in fact *is* the nature of the case. It is the answer to that question that on Farmer's own analysis turns out to be not *at all* self-evident.

4

I have not being trying to deny that people have momentous experiences that they believe can be described only by saying, 'I sense a personal presence, as of God. . . .' Many people do. Some of them take the sense as unquestionably reliable; others see the immense possibilities of misreading the experience and wish to protest when these dangers are ignored. We have been seeing how the language, analogies, and thought-models used by Brunner and Farmer fail to bring out how serious these dangers are.

Now if a philosophical or theological position is well secured (intellectually), it is not philosophically important to inquire

[1] *The World and God*, p. 158; italics mine.

what *psychological* pressures might by themselves lead one to that same position, to adopt those same beliefs, even in the absence of good rational justification. It is normally a sound policy to keep philosophical and psychological issues well apart. But because the 'analogy' between human and divine encounters is so weak, and because the 'sense of encounter' turns out to be a very fallible sense, it is impossible to brush aside as theologically irrelevant the views of those psychologists (particularly the Freudians), who deny that the 'divine–human encounter' can validly be taken as a meeting between two persons. To the Freudian, the voice of God is, in the end, our own voice, or the voice of aspects of our personality 'projected', unknown to ourselves, upon the cosmos at large. It is as if we shouted to the hills and took the echo to be the hills replying.

Farmer in *Towards Belief in God* queries the convincingness of the Freudian account of how exactly this projection occurs, the details of its mechanism. And he quite rightly points out that their arguments do nothing to discredit the belief that, projections apart, God may still as a matter of fact exist as a person: that in the midst of all the echoes (to develop our simile) we should recognize also a real voice calling to us.

But one could agree with Farmer, criticize the Freudian story in many details, and still be compelled to feel that it has disclosed something that must be peculiarly and deeply disquieting to the religious mind. It is this. Perhaps only those who have undergone psycho-analysis or have gained some facility in self-analysis can fully realize the extraordinary transformations that can happen to early experience, the weird remoteness and otherworldliness that clothe and disguise certain memories (of landscapes, people, objects) when revived in adult years. These memories seem quite discontinuous with our ordinarily remembered life-history, the people and places one recollects seeing and knowing. And yet in these cases we are nonetheless compelled finally to accept them as our memories, not as new experiences of a hitherto veiled 'other world' or as encounters with supernatural beings. We realize, as never before, the risk we so often run of misreading our experiences dramatically. A fragment of autobiography may illustrate this more vividly.

On several occasions widely spaced in time I dreamed of a landscape, which I had no memory of having actually visited. I stood on a high plateau, immense and flat beneath an intensely blue sky. There were no people to be seen, but strange bright columns surrounded me, clear-edged masonry like that of temples and towers. The dream brought a great sense of exhilaration, of having reached a place infinitely more worth lingering in than the humdrum localities of everyday life; and immeasurably remote from them all. My paradise-landscape lay neither north nor south, east nor west of any place on any map. It did not participate in the successiveness of time: its buildings were neither ancient nor modern; and I who watched them was neither young nor old. The details of the dream vanished on waking, but not the haunting sense of the 'numinous', the combined dread and exaltation of mind, which remained for some days. These dreams continued to puzzle me until a recent stay in Edinburgh.

While sitting reading on the Calton Hill I noticed an odd familiarity and unexpected impressiveness about one of the fantastic (and much maligned) monuments with which the hill is crowned. A gradual association of ideas led back to the dreams; although the place where I sat, in the middle of the city (admittedly a small plateau, and clustered with columns and an artificial temple), had nothing whatever of the atmosphere of my dream landscape. But the more I associated, the more convinced I became that the landscapes were 'geographically' one and the same.

But what of the transformation of atmosphere? The answer came by recalling that the first time I visited Edinburgh and that hill was as a very small child; a child to whom the monuments would have been frighteningly large, the hill immeasurably high and cut off from the world below. The impact of that experience was not blunted at the time either by the adult habit of keeping track of movements in space on the map of the mind, or by an adult's punctuation of time into hours and minutes. The original memory, sliding up in dream-imagery, brought with it that child's vision intact, very different from the adult response to any possible landscape, therefore not to be found on any travel; remote and unearthly: understandably so.

In being 'explained', the dream has not lost its interest or much of its value. But one lesson could not be dodged, that the transition from 'numinous awe' to 'therefore experience of the transcendent'—of the 'wholly other'—is far from a reliable one, cannot honestly be called immediate or self-authenticating. Again the religious man is entitled to say that my dream-memory may still be what I originally was tempted to take it as—some sort of 'intimation of immortality', in this case preserved from the clear vision of childhood. And he could be right. Only, my confidence that he may be right is weakened by realizing that even on a *sceptical* view a childhood memory might reassert itself in adulthood with precisely the same sense of remoteness and discontinuity. Also, I seem able to trace the line along which the child's unreflecting vision slowly changes into the adult's workaday vision, with a confidence which I cannot muster for threading the analogical movement from human encounters to encounters with the transcendent.

The relevance of the autobiographical illustration lies simply in this: that it shows how an experience, strongly religious in tone, seemingly *sui generis*, and in the last resort incommunicable, can come to be seen by the person concerned in altogether a new light, as an encounter not with the transcendent but with some buried element of his own early life, transposed, as it were, into a strange, unfamiliar key: but if unfamiliar, then still recognized as his own by an insight equally compelling and authoritative as the original judgement about its self-evident transcendent origin. If then *both* the religious experience *and* its re-interpretation can present themselves with the same degree of immediate compulsiveness, it seems to follow that attempts to confirm either view *must* step outside the felt experiences themselves and consider reflectively the pros and cons of each. And if this is so, the theologians' embargo on philosophizing about the religious encounter must once more be lifted. To veto all reflection in the sphere of personality as distorting and degrading 'speculation' is to ignore all the fallibility, ambiguity, uncertainty, which I have been labouring in this chapter to describe. But the sort of reflection necessary to discriminate between real and seeming encounters is not speculation in the grand sense. It is the clarifying, sharpening, and testing of the analogies used by people in speaking of their experiences, the examining of the logic of words like 'self-authenticating' in their various contexts, everyday and religious, and not least the honest and *imaginative* consideration of views like that of Freud and the Freudians.

This inquiry could not justly be accused of treating persons as objects, and blasphemously reducing God to a thing-at-our-disposal. It does not interpose any systems of ideas between the *I* and the *Thou*. Thus, I cannot follow Buber in declaring that 'cogitative truth means making the absolute into an object . . .',[1] provided that cogitation is simply concerned to answer the preliminary but important question, 'Am I or am I not in personal contact with someone?' For here cogitation is very much in place. We have seen that to be aware of someone as a personal subject involves knowing *about* that person (perhaps a great deal about him), although it does not entail giving our minds to the detailed *entertaining* of that knowledge Totally dismissing all ideas about the person would lead not to 'purification' of personal relations but to their elimination: hence the misleadingness of Buber's either/or—'What the philosophers describe by the name of God cannot be more than an idea. But God, "the God of Abraham", is not an idea'.[2]

[1] Martin Buber, *Eclipse of God* (London: Gollancz, 1953), pp. 44 f.
[2] *Ibid.*, p. 67.

CHAPTER FOUR
'ENCOUNTERS' (2)

———

S OMEONE (White) at this point might object.

White: You have failed to do justice to the fact that one does *not* need to know a great deal about a person in order to be able to encounter him personally. One need know very little indeed. Buber may yet be right: 'It is not necessary to know something about God in order really to believe in him'; one may still 'know how to talk *to* God', although not *about* him.[1]

We could imagine a situation (fantastic, but no matter) where we make contact with someone about whom we know practically nothing. We are told, say, by a person we trust, to go by night to the edge of a wood and to address someone whom we shall not see or hear. It will be to our advantage, nonetheless, to enter upon *I–Thou* relations with him. These will be *direct I–Thou* relations, free from any interposing of ideas or speculation, as we *have* no ideas about the person at all. What would prevent us from faithfully saying *Thou* into the darkness?

Black: Nothing would prevent us. But saying *Thou* is not establishing an *I–Thou* relation of the sort Buber describes. Think how far it would be from the relation of child to parent, friend to friend. Instead of meeting a unique personality, I am addressing simply 'the man in the dark'. Compare (on the score of *impersonality!*) 'the man who takes my train-ticket', 'the man who delivers the milk'. Buber himself sees that anyone who can be

[1] *Eclipse of God* (London: Gollancz, 1953), p. 40.

49

characterized as 'the man who . . .' is bound to be an *It* to us and not a *Thou*.

White: But your relation with him need not be impersonal, like your relations with ticket-collectors and milkmen. You might address him sincerely (as in prayer), appealing to him as a person, not as to some official in his official capacity.

Black: You might, I agree. But would that be enough to justify calling this an *I–Thou meeting*? Suppose the whole thing were a hoax, and no one was there in the dark. Your supplications would presumably still take place in just the same way, though they were reaching no one's ear. So your sense of encounter, if any, could not reasonably be taken as evidence that you really had met someone. Just how unnatural it would be to call this situation a 'meeting' comes out clearly if we imagine that some time later I find myself in the same room as the person I had addressed in the wood (presuming, this time, that it was *not* a hoax). 'I have spoken to you, but we have never met,' might be a natural remark to make. No: my speaking into the darkness cannot count for me in itself and at that moment as an encounter achieved. I may imaginatively supplement the situation, help to make my speaking into the dark less absurd, by picturing a figure in the shadows, by taking it on my friend's authority that there *is* someone there, and accepting his account of the man's appearance and character, etc. But if so, my 'encounter' experiences are parasitic upon those of my friend (or upon those of the people on whose authority *he* relied). It is assuredly neither direct nor self-authenticating.

White: Don't be too anxious! All your suggestions have their theological, constructive counterparts. 'Now we see through a glass, darkly, but then face to face' (the ultimate, 'real' meeting). Or take 'authority' and its near relative, 'tradition'. Aren't these concepts to which Christianity has persistently turned?

Black: Of course. But to develop a theology in which these were crucial would be to leave far behind the language of direct, immediate, self-certifying encounter with a personal God. Suppose I do accept on authority what my unseen hearer is like— presumably an account of his character—facts about him such as why he interviews candidates for his philanthropy in the dark, his physical features, and so on. Now imagine me reflecting quietly and carefully upon this supplementary data, trying to piece it together, to discover what manner of man it could refer to, if to any. If I kept finding contradictions, anomalies, in this account, if the images refused to fit together convincingly as images of one person, I might again murmur, 'Practical joke all the time'. Or at least I should be sadly puzzled over which of the two options to choose: either, (*a*) should I accept the description as indeed of a real person, although of an inconceivably odd one— relying entirely on my 'sense of encounter' and on my friend's authority, or (*b*) should I instead doubt or deny the reality of the encounter and decide that my sense of presence was illusory, because a (logically) impossible being has been described as over against me? And that is to say, no being at all. One thing I could *not* do would be to decide that, *whatever* the conceptual difficulties in the description, my original sense of encounter remained serenely untroubled and unchallenged by them.

But you see to what this line of thinking would commit the theologian? To accept it would mean abandoning the simplicity of 'self-authenticating encounter' and returning to the inquiry called rational theology, which seeks precisely to answer the problems of the paradoxes or contradictions that beset descriptions of the divine nature. Appeal to *I* and *Thou* certainly would not have led to the elimination of that study as superfluous or as degrading to God's personal status.

(Interrupting the dialogue, one might further clarify Black's conclusions by referring yet again to the analogy with the clashing explanatory models in the theory of light. Ostensive definition of 'light' is so straightforward an operation (as compared with the attempt at similar definition of 'God') that *no amount* of conceptual nightmares would make it reasonable to go back on one's confident claim, 'Of course, there is such a thing as light.' It is not nearly so certain that the combination of conceptual enigmas *and* the precariousness about interpreting any experience as of 'meeting God' could not make it reasonable to go back on one's claim, 'Of course, there is such a being as God.' Superficially the cases are parallel; but, in detail, they diverge alarmingly.)

White: It has just struck me that something quite vital has been left out of our conversation; something which, once reckoned with, may yet allow us to reinstate the theology of *I* and *Thou* to the place Buber and his followers have prepared for it The vital thing is *reciprocity*: a personal relationship must be *two-sided*.

Black: You mean the man in the dark would have to speak, after all, before we could be in personal relations with him?

White: He might speak through *events*—to keep our simile close to what believers say about God.

Black: —by delivering the philanthropic goods?

White: I suppose so: but that would seen to yield a very crude notion of God's reciprocal activity, if we translated our parable into the language of religion. We could not do better than return to Buber's way of putting it, that anything whatever in nature and history can become a manifestation of, or revelation of, God to the man who seeks God in it. Only, that does not mean that these events leave us with a detachable 'message'. They leave us with an enhanced sense of the meaning of life, with a sense of 'presence', but not with some specific 'content', which we could reduce to a formula. Now, *this* is not a mere speaking into the darkness and unresponding silence, even although we *still* are not being furnished with conceptual 'knowledge about' God.

Black: Right: then our task, as I see it now, will be to ask the question, 'Is it reasonable, appropriate, to *take* these experiences of enhanced meaningfulness and so on, *as* the divine reciprocity in action, as it were?' This is a question which, for thoroughness, we should have to follow out in dialogue with each *I–Thou* theologian in turn; for these share no common line in this matter. Since we shall have to be selective, let us stick to Buber. Let us ask, How plausible is *his* account of our recognition of God's reciprocity in personal relations?'

White: Well; Buber maintains that we can direct attention to both things and persons as *It*s or as *Thou*s. Where we see things or persons as *Thou*s, we can make out a scale of increasing reciprocity from our encounter with inert inanimates (reciprocity zero) through relations with animals, human beings, up to God, where reciprocity is realized to the full. . . .

Black: Stop there a moment. That is not *quite* accurate. For Buber says, doesn't he, that *everything* has its passive, disposable aspect *and* its active, personal aspect. Remember his famous (or notorious) account of meeting a tree as a *Thou*. The tree 'is bodied over against me *and has to do with me*, as I with it—only in a different way. . . . relation is mutual'.[1] We read also of the 'mute proclamation of the creature', of the cat through whose anxious gaze we momentarily meet (or think we meet) a *Thou*.

That is to say, reciprocity does not appear only at the levels of human and divine encounters. We cannot argue from the sense of reciprocity that we are over against a person as men are persons and as God is held to be personal. I find this worrying. Suppose there were no God: I could then, presumably, still address my tree, my cat, as *Thou*s. With enough imagination I might believe that I could address the universe as a whole as a *Thou*, and obtain the same sense of reciprocity as Buber calls experience of revelation.

White: But Buber sets himself resolutely against pantheism; and he locates the error of pantheism exactly here, that it thwarts the

[1] *I and Thou* (Edinburgh: T. & T. Clark, 1937), p. 8; italics mine.

two-way relationship between man and God. Perhaps there is the glimmer of reciprocity between men and things; but it is minute indeed compared with that between men and other men, men and God.

Black: My worry is not that he has forced himself into pantheism, but that an appeal to a sense of reciprocity cannot be relied on as Buber does rely on it to indicate—'person over against me'. This is because there is *so much* reciprocity in Buber's universe! Might we not make some ghastly mistake in imagining ourselves in communication with God, a God 'behind' the world, when in fact we had been *I–Thou*-ing aspects of the world itself, not the world's creator? How could we tell which we had been doing?

White: If in no other way, by the transformation effected in one's life by the encounter. I spoke of the enhanced sense of meaningfulness. . . .

Black: You would be saying that these effects are compatible only with God as their author, that no other explanation would be in principle possible? What, for instance, if it were claimed that the mere belief that one was contacting some supreme source of purpose in the world might produce (though wrong) just the same enhanced sense of meaning as if the belief were correct?

White: Oh, I could not rule out all sceptical explanations as necessarily impossible logically. But what right has either of us to demand logical necessity for our views?

Black: No right at all, I'll grant you. You would simply be saying that the religious account was the most *plausible*. Or am I still overstating?

White: I've no quarrel with that. If some other explanation proved to be more plausible, I should give up the theological one—or give up being intellectually honest.

Black: You have conceded all I need to make my point; which is this. We have seen already that the theology of *I* and *Thou*, far from displacing the traditional apologetic theologies (as it sometimes claims to do), itself stands in need of them to be able to cope with legitimate questions about the Being who is said to be over against me in the 'encounter'. ('Can a non-contradictory account be given of him?' is one such question.) We are now discovering that we run the risk of serious blunders unless we discriminate very carefully between different sorts of reciprocity, and that vital to this discrimination are rival explanations (philosophical, psychological) of the effects on the believer of his claimed encounter with God. In other words, we have a second inescapable apologetic task laid upon us, one which, again, cannot be shrugged off as 'objectifying' or 'degrading' God: nor can the theologian honestly say, 'Forget your doubts, yield to God in immediate, self-authenticating encounter': for if anything has been shown to be false it is just this claim to self-authentication.

White: I *do* encounter God directly, immediately; and the encounter *is* self-authenticating. If you cannot *verify* that, at least you cannot *falsify* it.

Black: I don't suppose I can. But if you had said that every solar system is really an atom in a vast super-universe, where they make up a cosmic cauliflower; that too would be both unverifiable and unfalsifiable: but still a very quaint belief.

Verification apart, we can still ask important questions about your statement. For one thing: *whom* did you say you encountered?—I mean *immediately* encountered.

White: God.—What else did Socrates expect me to say?

Black: What *sort* of God? There are Gods many and lords many.

White: I mean 'God the Father Almighty, Maker of heaven and earth. . . .'

Black: All right. Now what I should very much like to know is whether all this information about God is given in the immediacy of the encounter, and if so, how. For in one important sense of 'immediate' all that is given to one are certain sensations, from which in various ways and with varying degrees of fallibility we build up our world of things and persons. But how could one know *immediately* and certainly that God was Father Almighty, or that he made the heavens and earth . . .? But perhaps I see what is happening. Tell me this. Is 'God' a descriptive word, like 'manager', 'bishop', or is it a proper name like 'Mary' or 'James'? Or at least which of these does it most resemble?

White: Of the two, I should think it is far more like a proper name—one that applies uniquely to one person. Or, putting it another way, when I say 'God' I mean simply the *Thou* of my prayers. It is not a general term, anyhow; it doesn't refer to an impersonal office or function. Well, it *has* been used in that way: but if God is known authentically as *Thou* only, I should want to emphasize this by taking 'God' as the name of the *Thou* of prayer and as nothing besides.

Black: And yet you want to deny that there is any hazardous inference between saying, 'I encounter God', and saying, 'The being I encounter is Father Almighty, Maker of heaven and earth'! If 'God' were being used with descriptive force, then of course there is no difficulty in passing from the first statement to the second. For we should be using 'God' as *equivalent to* 'that being who is Father, who created . . . etc.'. But there *is* a difficulty, when God is taken as a proper name, or as the name of the *Thou* of prayer. For then to say that he is Father and Creator is to add new information about him that is not part of the meaning of the word itself.

Here is the crux. You wish at all costs not to distort your *I–Thou* encounter with God. This pushes you towards excluding descriptive elements from the word 'God'. But if you do exclude them, you cannot also consistently claim 'directness' and 'immediacy' for your judgements that the one you encounter is Father, Creator, and so on. What you are doing is giving an *illusion* of immediacy through oscillating between descriptive and proper-name uses of the word 'God'.

You pray, and address the *Thou* of your prayers as 'God' (proper-name use). Fair enough. In saying that you are speaking to God in this context, you are saying nothing whatever about any attributes which this being may possess. But you yield to the temptation of presuming that you are entitled to go on to assert that you have encountered 'God' (using the word now descriptively), '*the One who is Father Almighty . . .*' This punning, as we might call it, disguises the fact that some very bold and not at all self-certifying supplementation is taking place—supplementation of your actual given sense of encounter with an unseen *Thou*. So even if one grants that you have encountered a *Thou* in prayer, we shall still have to turn to reflection, perhaps to philosophical theology, to set about establishing the truth or falsity of the statements that this is God the Creator, the Infinite, Eternal Ground of Being.

White: I see: you are trying now to whittle down my original claim to encounter directly the God of the Christian faith to a statement about—I suppose—certain sensations I have, sensations that may or may not furnish reasons for believing in the reality of the *Thou* whom I trust I am meeting.

Black: The most I feel confident to say is that your claim can be made immune from falsification only by making it look suspiciously *like* a 'psychological' report, like 'I feel cold', 'I see as it were a blue star'.[1] But those judgements, unfortunately, win their immunity at the cost of saying nothing whatever about the world outside me. They speak the language of 'It seems to me as if . . .'

[1] Compare C. B. Martin, 'A Religious Way of Knowing', in *New Essays in Philosophical Theology*, ed. Flew and MacIntyre (London: S.C.M., 1955), pp. 76 ff.

never properly the language of 'encounter achieved' between myself and some other person.

White: Why could not statements about God resemble psychological statements in being immune from disproof, but be unlike them in that religious statements uniquely *do* describe contact with the 'not-ourselves', whereas the psychological ones never do this? [1]

It is the old point again: God is not a thing, therefore verification-tests suitable for things will give negative results when applied to God. . . .

Black: But there are *some* tests for the existence, presence, and activities of *persons*.

White: Tests that are inappropriate, however, in God's quite unique case. God has no *It* aspects. But the failure of all the tests doesn't show that there isn't a God.

Black: No: it doesn't provide any knock-down refutation, I agree. But can we allow experiences of encountering God to elude absolutely every checking procedure, without a grave risk of eroding away the original analogy altogether? Certainly, you can hold on to the language of encounter with God, the form of words and the claim; you can even hold on to a verbal shell of analogy. But what we do *not* seem to have found in all our discussion is how to discover which response is the more rational— the response of the believer, who still clings to his analogy and claims his encounter is with a real being, or that of the sceptic who decides that the analogy has broken down, and that the 'encounter' is illusory.

White: This may be a demand we have no right to make. Perhaps all the evidence is ambiguous, the religious and the sceptical responses *equally* rational or equally irrational. *Decision* for or against belief is required, not logical discrimination.

[1] See W. D. Glasgow, *Philosophy*, July 1957.

Black: Up to a point, the situation does look ambiguous. The Christian conscientiously objects to verification-tests for God's existence ('degrading', 'objectifying'). He rejects even the sort of checks we normally employ with persons, although God meets us in some way *as* a person: but a 'pure' person, which is different. [That notion of 'purity', we have seen, is odd and confused; but let it pass for the moment.] We notice, however, that in moving from crude verifiability and falsifiability to immunity from both, the believer is at the same time moving from a position where illusion would be detectable to one where it could be eternally concealed. He may (though this cannot be proved) be moving from using language to state what exists to using it merely to report his sensations or to evoke attitudes. Whether the believer reaches the end of those last two scales, and his claims thereby become wholly subjective, cannot, I should guess, be settled.

But it must not be forgotten that the balance swings evenly *only so long as the believer persists in speaking of 'self-authentication',* *'directness', 'immediacy'.* And we have seen reason to believe that this language is seriously misleading, that it illicitly denies the need for a rational theology as a supplement to the encounter-experience, whatever that is like. We have seen that questions *about* God cannot be kept from intruding by any *fiat*, and that in more than one connection. If those supplementations of the *I–Thou* experience prove unintelligible, internally incoherent, the entire logical situation is altered, and the balance goes down against the Christian view. Should they prove coherent, the reverse is the case.

The disheartening thing is that *I*-and-*Thou* theologians have been of all people the most strident in proclaiming that God's being and nature are quite *un*intelligible and opaque to human reason; that to the intellect he is irreducible scandal.

CHAPTER FIVE

MEANING AND MEDIATOR

————

I

IT would have been a neat and happy solution to the problems of theological paradox, if the attempt to 'single out' God in encounter had succeeded. While it is obviously true that we have not examined every version of theologies that make this attempt, nor given any knockdown demonstration that all must fail, still it is hard to see how any procedure could be suggested that would satisfactorily do for the God of Christianity what our pointings and touchings do so efficiently for finite objects and persons. Crucially, there could be nothing delimited about that God, which could allow one to identify him, saying, 'This *is* he; that is *not* he.' And yet the solution towards which these attempts move is such an attractive one, that it would be silly to abandon it entirely without asking whether any modifications could save it, even in part, and even at the cost of dropping the claims to directness and immediacy.

One can readily see what form one possible modification could take, if one considers certain statements of Jesus. 'He that hath seen me hath seen the Father.' 'I and my Father are one.' What these statements suggest is that pointing at Jesus might be 'as good as' pointing at God, and that to be able (as we are) to speak meaningfully about Jesus might mean that we are able to talk with equal meaningfulness about the acts and utterances of God. If this were true, then the paradoxes in the idea of God, the linguistic ruptures in our talk about him, would be no ultimate stumbling-

60

blocks to belief. We could confidently say that so long as we could believe in Jesus, we should logically be unable to lose belief in God. We might nickname this an 'indirect ostensive definition of "God" '. Instead of pointing at, or encountering, God himself, it is Jesus who is 'singled out'; and talk about God is translated into, or reduced to, talk about Jesus. Meaningful, non-paradoxical talk: good talk.

As a minor variation, the theologian could hold that talk about Jesus is a kind of linguistic half-way house on the way to talk about God. Jesus has often been called the 'Mediator': we should now be taking this to include the mediation of *meaning*. A more picturesque metaphor could be drawn from navigation, from the selecting of some visible landmark which one knows to be in a direct line with one's hidden objective. The landmark stands in as a reliable substitute for the unseen goal. To steer towards the landmark is to steer towards the objective. So, to set oneself on a course towards understanding Jesus is to be *ipso facto* set towards understanding God, although the attainment of that ultimate goal is beyond human capacity in this life at least. To know what Jesus meant by 'love' is to be on the right track towards discovering what God's love is. And so on.

A theology that stakes its all upon knowing God exclusively (or almost exclusively) through Christ is most often called a 'Christological' theology. In the present chapter we shall try to discover whether such an approach might succeed where the encounter theologies fail. The controlling questions will have to be these: Have those theologians justified their procedure (this reduction of all talk about God to talk about Jesus) without the risk of re-introducing in the course of their justification itself the contradictions and enigmas that we are hoping to escape? Have they made good their claim that the ultimate meaningfulness of speaking about God is guaranteed by our ability meaningfully to speak about Jesus?

2

There is no difficulty in finding examples of twentieth-century theologians who have given a central place to Christology. The most notable and most thorough specimens are the theologies of Karl Barth and those most influenced by him. But even within Catholicism, a number of theologians have been regarding the arguments of natural theology as no more than a preparation of the mind for the real message of Christianity—the doctrines concerning the Person of Christ. Protestant Christologies very often tend to repudiate the whole enterprise of natural theology, to reject all rational 'justifications' of belief, and in many cases to spurn metaphysics as decisively as any positivist. All is staked, therefore, on Jesus as the one who awakens faith, who reveals all that can be known and needs to be known of God. To 'awaken faith' is not to communicate some system of eternal truths about the world and God, nor to give some intellectually satisfying explanation of the human predicament. It is to become aware of oneself as confronted by a Person before whom one stands judged and is found wanting. Repentance and obedience are the imperatives, not intellectual understanding: self-committal to a way of life, not an objective scrutiny of the faith's credentials. The root error of 'speculation' is its love of *abstract* theory and *general* ideas. True Christianity concerns itself with the concrete, the unrepeatable, and the particular. It offers, not a philosophy of life, but a redeeming and forgiving Saviour, known only in the Word of God, which records his once-for-all incarnation. Accept that one vital claim—that in the New Testament God is to be seen 'reconciling the world to himself' through Christ, and at once our failures with metaphysics and philosophy of religion become quite unimportant, mere reminders of our finitude, and no hindrance to belief. True theology is *fides quaerens intellectum*, faith in search of understanding.

'A church dogmatics', Barth writes, 'must... be christologically determined as a whole and in all its parts.'[1] Hans Urs Von Balthasar, one of Barth's keenest interpreters, follows him in giving a crucial position to Christology: 'As centre of history and creation, Christ is the key not only to the interpretation of the world but also to the knowledge of God.'[2] To Professor T. F. Torrance, 'It is the incarnation of the Word which prescribes to dogmatic theology both its matter and its method.'[3] 'Christology', says Professor D. M. MacKinnon, is 'something that sets in motion and keeps in restless activity, the whole work of the characteristically Christian theologian.'[4] When it is added that Von Balthasar writes as a Roman Catholic, Professor Torrance as a member of the Church of Scotland, and Professor MacKinnon as an Anglo-Catholic, it is plain how widely disseminated this Christological movement has become.

In discussing the movement we shall be able only to select one or two of the main philosophical issues raised by it, ignoring the many real differences of opinion among the Christologists themselves, Barthians and non-Barthians, also the differences between the Barthians and *Barth*. Probably the majority of these theologians are committed, along with their Christo-centric views, to some version of the *I–Thou* encounter theologies. I think, all the same, that the fundamental problems of Christology and those of the encounter theories are logically distinguishable, and can be usefully discussed apart.

In a remarkable passage in his *Church Dogmatics*, Barth makes the general Christological standpoint both picturesque and more

[1] Karl Barth, *Church Dogmatics*, Vol. I, Second Half-Volume (English translation by Thomson and Knight, Edinburgh: T. & T. Clark, 1956), p. 123.

[2] Hans Urs Von Balthasar, *La Théologie de l'Histoire* (Paris: Librairie Plon, 1955), p. 28.

[3] Professor T. F. Torrance, 'The Place of Christology', in *Essays in Christology for Karl Barth* (London: Lutterworth Press, 1956), edited by T. H. L. Parker, p. 13.

[4] Professor D. M. MacKinnon, 'Philosophy and Christology', in *Essays in Christology*, p. 272.

precise than do those brief quotations. He describes the centre-piece of the well-known Isenheim altar by Grünewald. It concerns the Incarnation.

> In the background upon the heights of heaven, beyond earth's highest mountains, surrounded by innumerable angels, there is God the Father in His glory. In the foreground to the left there is the sanctuary of the old covenant. It also is filled with and surrounded by angels, but inexorably separated from the background by an immensely high, gloomy partition. But towards the right a curtain is drawn back, affording a view. And at this point . . . stands Mary as the recipient of grace . . . in adoration before what she sees happening on the right side. Over there . . . the child Jesus lies . . . a child of earth like all the rest. Only the little child . . . sees what is to be seen there, the Father. He alone, the Father, sees right into the eyes of this child. On the same side as . . . Mary appears the Church, facing at a distance. . . . What it sees directly is only the little child in His humanity; it sees the Father only in the light that falls upon the Son, and the Son only in this light from the Father. . . . It can only look out of the darkness in the direction in which a human being is to be seen in a light, the source of which it cannot see itself.[1]

But although this parable gives a new precision to the Christological view, it still does not give it precision enough for our purposes. For a start, we have to distinguish between what I shall label a 'strict' and a 'free' Christology. By a strict Christology I mean one that is prepared to follow out rigorously its belief that all statements about God are analysable without remainder into statements about Jesus. By a free Christology I mean one that is less thorough-going than that; one that holds that although there is very little we can sensibly say about God as he is in himself, and that although our knowledge of Jesus illuminates our knowledge of God, yet we are not so utterly dependent on statements about

[1] Barth, *op. cit.*, p. 125.

Jesus as the strict view maintains. Professor D. M. Baillie, for example, made Christology quite central to his thought: witness his book, *God was in Christ.* Yet Baillie thought one could ask meaningfully (*before* speaking about Jesus) what manner of God it was who was to become incarnate. Some writers argue that, whether or not God may be spoken of without linguistic breakdown, all we can *safely* say about him is what Jesus authorizes us to say. To speculate is to run the risk of introducing ideas and trains of associations that are quite foreign to the biblical thought-forms, and are bound to warp and twist the content of the revelation, when it is translated from the one idiom to the other.

Sometimes the intention in interpreting a doctrine along Christological lines is not so much to give meaning to the otherwise unintelligible as to give human relevance and imaginative sharpness to the remote and the hard to conceive. Thus the dimly grasped conception of God creating the world is given a new freshness and vigour by being brought into close relation with the 'new birth' or 'new creation' which Jesus came to make available to men. The link between the two creations is given an ultimate warrant by the doctrine of the Trinity and Christ's place in it. 'He is the image of the invisible God, the firstborn of all creation; for in him were all things created . . . through him and for him.' [1]

It is, however, the *strict* Christologists that are of real concern to this study. For it is only they who can say with some plausibility that they rely on no metaphysics and that, in the most fashionable manner, they follow 'the way of experience'.

We must now ask this: assuming we can point at, or single out, Jesus and speak of him meaningfully, how exactly are these procedures related to pointing at, singling out, and speaking about God himself? We shall then ask the still more fundamental question: how can the Christologist *justify* his assurance that to speak of Jesus is to speak in some way of God? Or, expressing this in

[1] The *Essays in Christology* to which I have referred contain a chapter by W. A. Whitehouse on 'Christ and Creation'.

terms of the Grünewald picture, how does Barth (and Grünewald) know that the painting is faithful to the facts, that it *correctly* delineates the relation between God the Father, Jesus Christ, and the believer? How can he account for his claim that his picture is no fantasy, but a dependable symbol of the real?

3

If we took *literally* the texts, 'He that hath seen me hath seen the Father', and 'I and my Father are one', they would seem to imply that God and Jesus were *identical*. But a little reflection shows that this would be immediately disruptive of several fundamental Christian ideas. For one thing, it would conflict with the doctrine of the Trinity. It would mean that when God became incarnate, he no longer dwelt also in eternity, but underwent a metamorphosis like any pagan deity. Second, this view would make nonsense of every sentence in which Jesus himself speaks of God and of his own relation to God: for if God and Jesus were identical, we should be at liberty to substitute for the word 'God' in these sentences, the word 'I' or 'me' etc. ('I will pray to the Father' becomes 'I will pray to myself'; 'The Father loveth the Son' becomes indistinguishable from 'I love myself'.) [1] Third, Christian thought has kept emphasizing Jesus' *humanity*: that is, it uses language in talking of him that could not be equally appropriate in talking of God. Jesus thirsts, hungers, is unaware of some coming events. In order for the Resurrection to be logically possible, he must be able to die. And none of these things can be said about God the Father.

So our texts do not give us licence (as superficially it seemed as

[1] It would be more accurate to say that this makes nonsense of all such sentences, *except* a sentence which *defined* or *established* the relation between Jesus and God. And this sentence would best be couched in what philosophers call 'the formal mode of speech': i.e. 'you may replace appearances of the word "God" by the word "Jesus", without change of meaning'.

if they did) to translate *without change* statements about Jesus into statements about God. God and Jesus may be related closely enough to allow indirect ostensive definition of some kind, but it will not be so simple a kind as it would be if God and Jesus were identical. It does not look as if there will be a 'one–one correlation' between attributes of Jesus and attributes of God. Something in God may answer to, say, Jesus' love and his power over nature, but nothing may answer directly to his finitude, his physical weariness, or to the fact that he could be tempted. With his characteristic boldness, Barth has claimed that Jesus is not particularly impressive, as a historical figure. One could mention more remarkable and more astonishing characters than him. And yet Barth also wants to say that theological problems concerning the nature of God are ultimately problems of Christology. Presumably God *is* particularly impressive, even although Jesus is not. Here then is the riddle: How can one at once *both* make Jesus one's sole guide to what can be affirmed about God, *and* insist that many things we say about Jesus may *not* properly be said about God also?

At this point I might be accused of largely manufacturing the difficulties through neglecting a supremely important distinction, the distinction between the name 'Jesus' and the title 'Christ'. Jesus may not be particularly impressive, but no one suggests that *Christ* is not. Jesus was subject to all the conditions of finite human existence, was born, lived in time and space, and was crucified; but to speak adequately of Christ we must call upon some very different language—to declare, for instance, that he shares from all eternity the life of the Godhead as the Second Person of the Trinity. Between the two expressions, 'Jesus' and 'Christ', there is all the difference between a common Jewish proper name and the unique title, 'the Anointed of God'. The gulf between the 'unimpressive' Jesus and God himself does not have to be spanned by the Christologist. It would require to be spanned only if he became a 'Jesusologist' instead.

This objection is worth making. It clarifies our task. But what it does *not* do is eliminate any difficulties from Christology. It is true that if I can speak meaningfully of Christ, I can *ipso facto* speak meaningfully about God. But this does not record a theological victory; it follows simply from the way we use the word 'Christ'. For we *mean* by 'Christ' the Son of God, and thus in using the word at all accurately we *presuppose* that the phrase 'Son of God' makes good sense, and therefore that the word 'God' itself makes good sense. But a theology that presupposes this is not the theology we are trying to study. We are turning to Christological theologies in order to be able, if possible, to conclude at the end of our study that talk about God makes sense, and that Christology has shown it makes sense. So it will not do to start off by *presupposing* that it makes sense.

If you like, the gulf we are really worried about is the gulf between 'Jesus' and 'Christ' rather than that between 'Jesus' and 'God'. How do we pass from the historically relative, hungering and thirsting Carpenter of Nazareth to the Person of the Trinity by whom and through whom 'the worlds were made'? Again, this is no mere logic-chopping. The complacent slurring across from one name to the other, and even more the uncritical use of the amalgam of the two, 'Jesus Christ', is one of the reasons why so many officially strict Christologists make their task seem easier than it is by quietly slipping into a free Christology at awkward moments. They are not resolute in reducing talk about God to talk about the Carpenter. The justifying of our indirect ostensive definition must lie in showing that it is reasonable to take statements about God as logically yoked to statements about Jesus, the Jesus to whom we can after a fashion gesticulate. This question is begged, not solved, by accepting *as something 'given'* the equation 'Jesus is the Christ'.

We are seeing here what is perhaps the chief hazard to which a thorough-going Christology is exposed. It is the temptation upon the theologian to supplement illicitly his knowledge of God by what has *not* been strictly derived from knowledge of Jesus. This is a special case of that recurrent danger to which David

Hume drew memorable attention. In his discussion of 'Providence' he argued that if we are, for instance, relying exclusively on a proof of God from the design, signs of purpose, marks of benignity found in the world, we are entitled to claim that the God who made all these is himself *as* cunning, *as* morally good, and so on, *as these evidences warrant*. But we are not entitled to say more. We have no right to say that the design is fragmentary, but God is the author of a faultless plan, of which we are seeing only a corner. We have no right to say that despite the evil and the suffering he is morally perfect. These may be true statements, but they cannot be elicited from those evidences alone.[1] So with strict Christology. We must ask (as Christologists themselves so seldom do), has the theologian really derived his conclusions from his talk of Jesus, or only in conjunction with extra, surreptitiously introduced *non*-Christological premisses?

4

In the essay on 'Philosophy and Christology' that I have already quoted, Professor D. M. MacKinnon puts forward an attractive and logically neat suggestion about the relation between God and Jesus—or (more accurately) about the relation between the languages in which each is spoken of. Although the terms he uses are drawn from recent analytic philosophy, the position he uses them to interpret is very close indeed to that of Barth.

There is certainly a note of positivism [in Barth], something analogous to that sounded by Bertrand Russell when he said, suggesting the application of the methods of mathematical logic to the solution of classical philosophical problems: 'Whenever possible, let us substitute logical constructions out of the

[1] 'If the cause be known only by the effect, we never ought to ascribe to it any qualities, beyond what are precisely requisite to produce the effect.' See *An Enquiry concerning Human Understanding*, Sect. XI, para. 105.

observable for inferred, unobserved entities.' There is in Barth something analogous to this recommended logical economy. We must, he insists, substitute for abstract general statements concerning the being and purposes of God, and of men, statements that show them in terms of, or set them in relation to, Jesus Christ.[1]

Philosophers who took Russell's hint found numerous applications for the idea of logical constructions, especially in the 'theory of knowledge'. Material objects might be thought of as logical constructions out of the raw material that the senses provide—the patches of colour, the data of sound and smell. Difficulties in the idea of the 'state' might also (it was hoped) be eliminated by conceiving the state as a logical construction out of its members. Why not then see our talk of God as a logical construction out of our talk about Jesus, our doctrines of sin and redemption as logical constructions out of the events of Jesus' life and ministry? To import this notion from philosophy would be a service to clarification, without destroying the real independence of theology. It has also the merit that it does not on the one hand assert that Jesus and God are simply identical, nor yet that any supplementation must be brought in from speculative philosophy, in order to pass from the one language-level to the other. Tables and chairs are not sense-data, but they are equally not sense-data *plus* some unsensed additional factors. Or so it was held.

But in general philosophy the notion of logical construction has had a far from successful career, a career that is bound to give one misgivings when we try to foresee its theological usefulness. Both the examples mentioned—the 'construction' of the state out of its members and the 'construction' of material objects out of sense-data—gave unexpected and serious trouble when detailed attempts were made to show how the constructing actually took place. The most elaborate accounts of the relation between the sense-data and the objects still seemed to leave a stubborn gap

[1] *Essays in Christology*, p. 284.

between claims to have these sense experiences and claims to be aware of the corresponding objects. There seemed no smooth way of passing from 'It seems to me as if there were a reddish patch with such-and-such shading' to 'I can see an apple.' It was impossible to decide exactly what sets of sense-data should be accepted as sufficient to *justify* a claim about a material object. One did not involve oneself in *contradiction*, if one asserted that *despite* all the (sense-datum) appearances there really was no apple there. Although, of course, this might be a very *odd* thing to say. Even with constructing states out of members, trouble was met. Some things can be said about states that we seem unable to express in terms of the behaviour of their members, however elaborate the experiments in translation we may carry out.

The reasons for those failures cannot be discussed here:[1] but the moral to be drawn from them is clear and relevant to the Christological venture. *In rough outline* the logical construction theories looked promising and even common-sensical. Only when the attempts were made to make them good *in detail* did the flaws appear. Thus, the initial appeal of their theological counterpart must not lead us to premature optimism.

Perhaps the prospects for its success or failure will become clearer in this new context, if we work out a little of the detail involved. I shall take the Christological treatment of the problem of evil as a serious and representative example.

Following Barth, D. M. MacKinnon writes, 'The problem of the evil will is the problem of Judas Iscariot.'[2] The problem of evil is not an abstract speculative problem. It is not to be dealt with in terms of impossibly general judgements about the relative amounts of suffering and happiness in the universe, or about evil as (sometimes) leading to good. 'This concentration on Iscariot is

---

[1] For a lucid account of them, see J. O. Urmson, *Philosophical Analysis* (Oxford, 1956), especially pp. 148 ff. Urmson's example of the difficulties involved in translating 'England declared war in 1939' into statements about the members of the state concerned, is particularly relevant.

[2] MacKinnon, *loc. cit.*, p. 282.

in no sense an illustrative device; it is justified because he is the place where the problem is raised with archetypal and definitive seriousness.' [1] If we can keep our attention focused upon his story alone in all its concreteness, we can leave unresolved and unresolvable the paradoxes raised by the traditional statements of the problem: the paradox of God's omnipotence and the presence of evil in the world, the paradoxes of predestination and freewill. We turn instead to the empirical and the concrete, to the words of Jesus at the Last Supper: 'The hand of my betrayer is on the table beside me! The Son of man moves to his end indeed, as it has been decreed, but woe to the man by whom he is betrayed!' [2] All that the theories tried to say about evil can be regarded as 'logically constructed' out of these words.

It is not an entirely unfamiliar move in discussions on moral issues to point at some concrete incident or event and say, '*That* tells you more about the problem than any general formula could.' A pessimist might say, 'If you want to know what life is really like, look at the child with cancer of the retina. If you speak of benevolent design, consider the cunning adaptation of the malarial parasite, the tubercle bacillus, the liver fluke.' [3]

There are, however, ways of contesting that kind of appeal. It can be rational or irrational—in some sense of these words. We can call those appeals one-sided, unrepresentative in their selection of cases. If sufficient counter-instances can be produced, the appeals can fail, or at least be shown to be little more than the expression of moods and biases. This would seem to imply, however, that if we could set alongside the Judas story sufficient *other* stories that conflicted with it, the Judas story itself would be displaced from the position the Christologist has given it. In fact, the Christian would never agree to this. No matter what cases were brought to his notice, he would say, '*Were it not for the Judas story*, I should not be able to avoid pessimism. For it looks

---

[1] MacKinnon, *loc. cit.*, p. 283.   [2] Luke 22. 21 f., Moffatt's translation.
[3] See, notably, Sir Charles Sherrington, *Man on his Nature* (Pelican edition, 1955), pp. 272 ff.

as though evil *does* often have the initiative, and keeps the initiative, and that there is no final guarantee that good can regain it in the end. But the story of Judas is the answer to all these anxieties. Judas seemed to wield the evil initiative, to flaunt it even before Jesus, and to have Jesus put to death. And to all appearances he was successful. Yet all the time the initiative had never properly been his at all, but had always remained with Jesus. All the evil instigated by Judas was used at every stage by Jesus in the furthering of his redemptive mission for all men.'

Can the Christian *justify* those very special claims he is making for the authority of this particular story? It is not easy to see a way of doing so—without being disloyal to a strict interpretation of his words, 'The problem of the evil will *is* the problem of Judas.' The Christian in fact gives the story its centrality, because he believes that the relation between Jesus and Judas is not just one more specimen human conflict, but that it reveals and symbolizes a concern on God's part for the deliverance of men from their sin. It involves believing that it is not only in this particular situation that God retains the benign initiative, but that he is omniscient, omnipotent, and therefore capable of entering creatively into human activities without himself being immersed in time or space.

It is not that our Christological interpretation of the Judas story has shown us how to overcome the paradoxes involved in speaking of God in these terms. On the contrary, what we are seeing is that the meaningfulness of such talk has to be presupposed before the Christological interpretation can get under way. Without it, the Judas story remains only one local and temporal instance of evil seemingly triumphant, but actually deflected to good: and counter-instances might prove it to be very untypical. Even that would be saying too much. For unless the betrayal and crucifixion are taken as phases in a total drama that culminates in the sitting of Jesus at God's right hand in heaven, it is far from obvious that the evil Judas did *was* deflected to good. And so the sceptic is entitled to stand the whole argument on its head. First he recognizes that those speculative and linguistically odd claims about God are in fact entailed by any acceptance of the Christological account of evil in terms of Judas and Jesus: but, secondly, these presuppositions are unacceptable, because of the paradoxes they contain. Therefore, the Christological interpretation that implies them is invalid.

This may be so, and yet MacKinnon was surely saying something of importance when he wrote, 'This concentration on Judas is not an illustrative device; it is justified because he is the place where the problem is raised with archetypal and definitive seriousness.' Certainly he was. The story of Judas is much more than a lecturer's 'example', one of the many that might equally well make his 'point'. Far more pregnant and memorable than any example are the parables, powerful symbols, and myths which can add imaginative vividness, wide suggestiveness, with economy of word and idea, to the bare logical scaffolding of the illustration or instance.[1] Judas belongs without doubt to this second group. But I can agree with MacKinnon that the story of Judas falls quite outside the sphere of illustration and still deny that the problem of Judas *is* the problem of evil. There is no *either/or* here: either the story is a mere illustration or else a concrete realization of the problem. The third and acceptable option is that the story is a vivid myth. (My use of 'myth' does not imply that it is historically false.) Only, in taking it this way, it becomes clear that it still stands in need of justification: we are entitled to ask, 'Why take *this* story as symbolizing the human situation *vis-à-vis* evil?' To answer that, we must do what the Christologist refuses to do, step outside the symbols and the myths. And when we do, I have argued, we are immediately confronted with those very ideas and concepts, which we hoped would be made meaningful for us by the Christologist.

(It is possible, however, for a Christian to accept the story of Judas as the answer to the problem of evil—solely *on the authority*

[1] I have developed these themes in my paper 'Vision and Choice in Morality' in the Aristotelian Society Supplementary Volume XXX, pp. 14 ff.

of Jesus. He might argue that we do not have to emerge from the myth at this point to speak of God's omnipotence, omnipresence, etc., as I am assuming. We remain *within* the myth from the time we accept Jesus as our authority. That is the supreme decision; and its rationality or irrationality becomes the supreme question. My final chapter considers this viewpoint at slightly greater length.)

I do not think that the difficulties uncovered in the Christological account of evil would arise only in the context of that particular problem. They are symptoms of what looks like a very general debility in the whole enterprise—in the theological application of logical constructions. Putting this in a rough-and-ready, non-technical way: We may grade the various claimants to the title 'logical construction' in a provisional order of plausibility. For instance, we might say that processions are clearly constructions out of people with banners and flags, decorated lorries, and the like. Enumerate these items, and you have described the procession. When your enumeration is finished, nothing is left over: the procession has no independent, mysterious existence over and above the people and things that comprise it. Second: it is not *quite* so plausible to say the same things about physical objects and sense-data: although it is not by any means *absurd* to attempt it. We might note, however, the sort of objection a philosopher in the Kantian tradition would make to the attempt. He would say that when you have listed any amount of sense-data you like, you would never have, *ipso facto*, described a physical object. When the listing was finished, something vital *would* have been left over, notably the idea of the *objectivity* of the physical object, something that is not given with any combination of sense-data and cannot be reduced to sense-data. Third: it looks to me most *im*plausible to say that once we have spoken of certain historical events in first-century Palestine, of certain finite things and persons, that we have *ipso facto* described God: that when our enumeration of these has ended, nothing essential is left over. For, unlike the procession, God, if God exists, most certainly *has* an independent, mysterious existence over and above all those events. And yet it is to reduce talk about God to talk of the events (in particular the event of Jesus) that the logical construction experiment is invoked.

Expressing this in more formally theological jargon: the whole force of calling God 'transcendent' (as the Christian does and must) is to insist above all else that *no* set of finite, historically relative events *could* stand to God in the same way as the torch-bearers and the decorated lorries stand to the procession. In the light of this, the task the Christologist set himself begins to look an impossible one. For it is the task of conjuring transcendence out of immanence, infinity out of finitude, eternity out of time.

One further example may help to bring home the magnitude of the problem. 'Conjuring eternity out of time' would be one way of describing what Von Balthasar tries to do in his discussion on Christ and time in *La Théologie de l'Histoire*. He holds that it is not by denying or reading out the role of time in the life of Jesus, that we can learn the meaning of eternity, but on the contrary by *stressing* the temporal, its importance in that life, the waiting for the 'hour' that should come, the moment-by-moment dependence of Jesus on God's will. 'Time is the form chosen by Christ (and thus adequate) for manifesting the true eternity.' [1] 'What makes Christ the Son from all eternity is the uninterrupted reception of all he is . . . as a gift coming from God.' [2] This could be accepted as a profound interpretation of these aspects of the life of Christ, *provided that* we were already confident that we could give a satisfactory meaning to 'eternal', 'eternity'. In that case, we should be able to say, 'These aspects of Jesus' life give the most accurate presentation of the eternal, that is possible within time.' But that would *not* be the same as logically constructing 'eternity' talk out of talk about time, as the strict Christological programme requires. It looks as if the facts to which Von Balthasar draws atten-

[1] Von Balthasar, *op. cit.*, p. 28.
[2] *Ibid.*, p. 33 (both quotations slightly paraphrased).

tion would remain no more than interesting and probably unique *temporal* patterns, unless we *did* explicitly or implicitly have some sort of independent idea of eternity, an idea that those New Testament facts express in terms of time, but that is not *itself* an idea of time. In other words, I do not see how we can *take* those aspects of Jesus' life as the most accurate presentation of the eternal, without bringing to our interpretation of them the undeniably metaphysical idea of eternity itself. If the Christological theologian denies this, then he must do what he has not hitherto succeeded in doing, namely, show exactly how he envisages the logical constructing of 'eternity' language out of 'time' language to take place; provide, as it were, an architect's plan of the construction. He has to show *why* Christ's 'waiting for the hour', his obedience to God, the reception of all he is as a gift, why these are not adequately described in temporal language, but cry out for a further description in terms of eternity revealed.

The demonstration of how the constructing is done, in detail, is a far more urgent task here than it is in those parallel experiments in general philosophy, where material objects and states are to be constructed out of sense-data and members. For in both these latter cases we know (or think we know) the materials, the bricks, with which the construction is to be done, and we also know the finished artefacts themselves, the material objects and the states. The only 'unknown' is the detailed means by which the constructing is achieved. The theological case is clearly not at all closely parallel to this. Here the artefact is unknown as well as the process of construction. We are unable to say clearly *what* we are constructing or how the ingredients come together to fashion it.

At the beginning of the chapter I used an illustration from navigation or path-finding in order to outline the aims of Christology. The Christian theologian believes that talk about Jesus is 'on the way to' talk about God: the former gives a bearing upon the latter as a landmark may put a traveller precisely on the line of his hidden objective. Von Balthasar says, 'The letter is not important . . . except in so far as it lets us *move on to* the spirit: the finite character of concepts, images, human words etc. . . . except in so far as allowing us access to the infinity of the divine Word.'[1] Would this analogy fare any better than the 'logical construction' approach?

The traveller requires not only a direction-mark but also a reason to believe that his objective exists and that it lies in the same line with the mark. If he does not at any moment see the two together, the landmark and the goal beyond it, he must go on the authority of the map-maker or the guide for believing both in the existence of the object and in its alignment with the mark that *can* be seen. We should not trust *any* map of *any* district, or the word of any self-styled guide. We properly invoke criteria, discriminating among the reliable and unreliable maps and guides. If it is asked 'Whence comes the authoritativeness of the Christological claim that talk about Jesus gives reliable lines of direction to talk about God?' the typical Christological answer is this: 'The revelation is reliable, because it is God's revelation.' But look at that answer. Consider the difficulties in trying to establish it as true. For within the terms of strict Christology, the word 'God', which appears crucially in the answer, is given sense by being taken as one of the hidden 'objectives' to which statements about Jesus (the biblical landmarks) are said to point reliably. But it is just the reliability of those landmarks that we are attempting to vindicate. The attempt proves to be circular. Christology cannot be vindicated along those lines, if it can be vindicated at all.

In the following section we shall make a new start, and try to deal more thoroughly with this vexing question of justification.

5

Often the most searching question to ask about any system of reasoning is, 'Does it leave room for the possibility of establishing

[1] Von Balthasar, *op cit.*, p. 142, my italics.

itself?' Or (negatively), 'Does it contain arguments by which it is itself shown to be invalid—or at least unverifiable?' An example of such a system would be a metaphysical theory that argued that there could be no valid (or meaningful) metaphysical theories. Being one itself, it would come under its own condemnation. . . . How would Christological theology respond if this question were applied to it? Can it give, in other words, a consistent and reasonable account of how it could be true?

In the Grünewald painting the believers are screened off from the open vision of God. They are able to see only the human Jesus; and if God is to be known to them, he is to be known only through what Jesus 'reflects' of him. Grünewald and Barth are believers. They belong, therefore, to the company of those whose vision of the divine is limited to their vision of Jesus. But Grünewald's painting is *not* a view of Jesus as seen from the stance of the believers. In the painting there appear the believers, Jesus, and the realm of God itself. How, we may ask, does Grünewald *get into* this uniquely privileged position? How has he emancipated himself from that restriction on vision which he shows to be imposed universally upon believers? Stating the problem in terms of the questions with which we began: 'Has not Christology made it impossible for itself to assert its own most important claim— the claim that the relation between God, men, and Jesus is what it says it is?' For if that claim is taken seriously, it implies that men are not in a position to know whether it is well founded or not.

As we have seen, the ultimate answer most Christologists are prepared to give to the question is this: 'We are sure about our claim because it is thus that the Word of God reveals the situation to be.' To go beyond that affirmation, they feel, is both pointless and presumptuous. To quote Barth: 'In Christology the limits as well as the goal [of thought and language] must be fixed as they are seen to be fixed already in the Evangelists and apostles themselves.'[1] The uniqueness of the subject-matter 'must also

[1] Barth, *op. cit.*, p. 125.

signify for us the boundary beyond which we are not to think or speak'. To Torrance, Jesus is the lord of our theological knowledge: 'As the Word become man, He is the criterion of our knowing.'[1]

All this is the most solemn rejecting of any attempt to confirm or criticize or challenge the central Christian claim, which the Grünewald painting symbolizes. It works its way into a theological theory of *truth* as essentially a matter of consistency or coherence with the main articles of belief.

This is a strange touchstone of truth. For it is obvious that a religion could be quite consistent or coherent, and yet entirely false. Any number of systems of belief could be constructed, given some imaginative agility, which would all pass the coherence-test but which could not all be true, since they clashed one with another in what they said about the world and the god or gods they believed in. But the coherence-test by itself could not tell us which of them was the true one, and which were false. Without using some other, independent test, there could be nothing decisive to choose between them. And yet Christians obviously believe that there is a *great deal* to choose between, say, Mohammedanism, Buddhism, and their own faith. They have often backed up their judgement by appeals to the historicity of the Resurrection, the remarkable moral and psychological effects of belief, by arguments that declare that God is 'demanded' as an explanation of the world's existence. But the type of theology with which we are now concerned tends to despise all these appeals; and many of its adherents even reject the whole idea of appeals—of no matter what kind. Barth denies that the grounds for his belief in Christianity as the revealed truth lie in any features that Christianity possesses as a religion, which other religions do not possess. At the level of 'features' or 'effects' Christianity does not stand out from its rivals in such a way as to justify its supreme claims for itself. Christianity is different only in that God has chosen to speak effectively

[1] Torrance, *op. cit.*, p. 17.

through it alone. It has been 'adopted' by God as the vehicle of his revelation.[1]

Barth illustrates his point. Half the earth receives light from the sun and half is in darkness. Which half is illuminated depends not on any features of that portion of the earth's topography: in neither half 'is there anything in the earth itself to dispose it for the day'.[2] So the light of God's judgement falls on the Christian faith, although nothing in Christianity 'makes it suitable for the day of divine righteousness and judgement'. 'For the Christian religion is true, because it has pleased God, who alone can be the judge in this matter, to affirm it to be the true religion.'

It is plain that the more single-mindedly Barth rejects the assessing of religions by reference to their 'features', and the more he denies that Christianity is distinctive, stands out decisively above the others and so on, the more heavily he has to rely on the affirmation that 'God has adopted Christianity'. But that affirmation is itself a piece of the Christian structure of belief, expressed (in true Christological fashion) in terms of God's forgiving of sinners and their adoption to sonship. Therefore, unless Barth were prepared—as he is *not*—to look for external, independent confirmation of the claim 'God has adopted Christianity', that claim, along with all else in Christianity, becomes simply one 'feature' of one religion among many. But the Christian cannot acquiesce in letting this crucial affirmation become only one of countless equally unassessable religious data. And yet, on his own showing, Barth can give it no *other* status without leaving the circle of biblical theology, and seeking independent confirmation for it.

The problem could be put as a version of the 'falsification' challenge discussed in Chapter One. We are asking Barth what would have to happen for him to change his mind about his affirmation that Christianity and no other is the God-adopted

---

[1] 'In itself and as such [Christianity] is absolutely unworthy to be the true religion. If it is so, it is so by election . . .' Barth, *op. cit.*, p. 352.

[2] *Ibid.*, p. 353.

faith. In what circumstances would he change his mind and opt, say, for Islam? How would he tell that *this* now was the chosen Faith? On his own avowal, it could not be that he had detected different *features* in those religions from what he had thought them to have before, nor differences in their psychological or other impact. In fact, Barth gives us *no* clear or consistent reply to this kind of question. The nearest to it is an appeal to the 'leap of faith'. There can be no communicating between the circle of theological ideas and experiences and anything *outside* that circle: no smooth path for argument from the one to the other. Attempts to find such a path are misconceived. We need, not an argument, but a jump.

This requires some comment. I do not think, first, that *every* Christological theology must go Barth's way here. One could argue that Christianity *is* decisively different from all the others; and justify this claim by reference to the total impact made upon one by the New Testament lives of Jesus and the witness of the early Church to him. One could say either that this impact is analysable or else *un*-analysable, for instance in psychological terms. In any case, it would be an impact such as to back up the judgement, 'This man speaks with absolute authority.' Everything else would naturally depend on the truth or falsity of that judgement.

Second, there are two contrasted kinds of response we can make to Barth's own 'leap of faith' view. The one response is to acclaim the frank way it replaces argument by conversion and shows up the notion of 'justifying' Christianity as irrelevant. The other response dubs the leap of faith 'irrational' in the bad sense, a final reason for choosing instead some way of life and thought from which reason has *not* abdicated, as it has from Christianity.

How can one arbitrate between these conflicting responses? There is something in this choice itself that gives it the appearance of a leap also! The sceptic may have to make his leaps as well as the Christian, and if so he cannot dismiss the Christian's position as absurd simply because it involves leaps. If he has a case against the Christologist it will have to be supplemented in some way or other. And the most tempting way of supplementing it would be by pointing out that even if the Christologist *can* escape from the task of 'justifying' his central affirmation, he still has not succeeded in detail in showing how to move safely from statements about Jesus to statements about God. If we are to make leaps, they might as well be in the direction of the positions that make the most sense to us. If ultimate justification is unattainable, there is all the higher a premium upon intelligibility.

6

Intelligibility, however, is not a claim that the Barthian often makes on behalf of the language he uses. Rather, he tends to flaunt its paradoxes and seeming nonsense, without realizing how ill he can afford to do so.[1] If he had *successfully* shown how talk about Jesus adds up to talk about God, and if he had found himself *able* to justify his judgement that in Christianity God reveals himself to men authentically, then the paradoxes would not matter. We should have 'indirectly ostensively defined' God as we had planned. But since neither of these tasks has been fulfilled, the troubles about meaning resume their old seriousness.

It will not do to evade that trouble by making either of two very popular moves. In the one case the theologians admit that the language of faith is ultimately unintelligible, to all, that is, but believers. It differs from ordinary language in that it makes sense only to some people, but not to all. This has a reasonable sound to it, but it relies on a muddled notion of how religious language works. The offending concepts are quite certainly part of the

[1] Exceptions, I know, could be quoted. Now and then Barth and Barthians vehemently deny that this language is strained or odd. But they far more commonly admit it.

English language—'God is a personal being, but not in time and space . . .' and so on. Independently of any religious commitment one can state as precisely as one wishes where the linguistic strains arise, the clash, for instance, between many of the implications of 'personal being' and of 'out of time and space'. It is true that commitment to Christianity or religious experiences following upon it might lead to so strong a sense of encounter, that God's existence would be taken as certain, and the paradoxes then ignored as trivial embarrassments only. But the person who did this would not have given meaning to what was formerly senseless or contradictory. The *linguistic* situation would be exactly as before, the clashes and conflicts of meaning unchanged.[1]

Again, it has been said that the language of Christianity *is* nonsensical, as the sceptics have shown—only, it is 'a nonsense that God uses' as the channel of his grace. We do not really know what we are saying in uttering it, but it is no less effective and authoritative for that. This suggests a view of religious language closely parallel to the view we have just been discussing with regard to God's 'adoption' of the Christian religion itself. But it is obvious at a glance that such a view would be quite unrealistic and artificial when judged against the sort of way the theologian himself uses that language. Theological language is, once more, continuous with *ordinary* language. It is not a nonsense language made up of senseless sounds, nor is it ever in fact treated in this way by theologians. It is also no magic language, providing 'open sesame' formulas for securing salvation. Theologians discriminate between acceptable and unacceptable formulas on the basis of what meaning they seem to have—not on the basis of the effects of uttering them. And of course if it *were* taken in this last, magical way, its dependence on observed effects would violate the Barthian embargo on all such tests.

Finally, a number of theologians use against the sceptic an argument more caustic than any I have yet discussed. It consists

[1] See also the discussion of these points in Alasdair MacIntyre's essay in *Metaphysical Beliefs* (London: S.C.M., 1957), pp. 175–9 ff.

in taking his worries and doubts over meaning and verification as no more than the manifestation of his sin. Doubt is *never* honest; and what are paraded as intellectual worries are in fact culpable refusals to admit the existence and the claims of God. Thus, the most innocent request for theological justification and the most earnest inquiry about how the theological senses are related to everyday meanings can be deflected as so many proofs of hard-hearted faithlessness. This implies that the theologian has no obligation to meet the doubter on his own ground, to argue with him seriously and in detail. All he can properly do is to pro-claim the Word to him in the hope that he will cease to doubt. As for the doubter himself: 'Everyone who has to contend with unbelief,' writes Barth, 'should be advised that he ought not to take his own unbelief too seriously. Only faith is to be taken seriously.' [1]

Some plausibility is given to this most unattractive argument by the insistence that belief consists not in accepting information about the world or God, but in entering upon particular kinds of relations with the divine *Thou*. It is a change in personal relations —from rebellion to obedience, not an assent to propositions. Nevertheless, as we saw in the last two chapters, this division be-tween *meeting* and *knowing about* is not nearly so sharp as *I—Thou* theologians most often assume. If it is true that I have an obliga-tion to enter upon relations of obedience with someone, it is true only if the relevant person exists. For I cannot have a duty to do something which is not in my power to perform. But what if I *am* unsure about God's existence? This doubt, I shall be told, is *par excellence* the blinding effect of sin. But I can ask the theologian why he believes what he has just said, namely that my unbelief results from sin. If he produces evidence, I can accept it on its own merits if it is adequate, and reject it if it is not. And in making up my mind to accept or reject it, nothing but the impartial scru-tiny of that evidence will be relevant. But suppose I reject it as insufficient, and suppose the theologian says that my rejecting of

[1] Barth, *Dogmatics in Outline* (London: S.C.M., 1949), pp. 20 f.

it is just one further manifestation of sin, then I can press him to tell me the evidence for this *new* assertion of his. I shall also point out to him that he has fallen into a vicious infinite regress, from which he can extricate himself only by admitting that at *some* stage, at *some* level, one's decision must be *upon evidence alone*. But if he admits this, he has surrendered his original position with regard to unbelief and sin. For the *ultimate* questions about whether or not to be a Christian will not have turned out, after all, to be properly dealt with by appeal to a duty to believe.

There are further complexities and confusions well worth studying in the use of the proposition 'Unbelief is the result of sin' and its near-neighbours. One interpretation might be that cowardice or fear or pride prevent people seeing the truth about Christianity, and not genuine intellectual difficulties. This would be a moral point. But to follow it through would again involve the Christologist in pointing out the features of Christianity that are being missed or misunderstood because of those moral deficiencies. This he will not do.

Or again, 'You ought to believe in God' could be taken as a properly moral imperative, concerned with an obligation to live out the Christian way of life, a life which the Christian believes is impossible without belief in God. But if I assented to this, would I be doing any more than setting myself to act *as if* there were a God? And would not my obligation be more accurately described as a duty to act as if God existed? But the theologian does not wish to speak of 'as ifs', but of outright, firm belief.

How does this doctrine of a duty to believe work itself out in practice? By appealing to it, a Christian is able (with an untroubled conscience) to reject anything that looks likely to disturb his faith, and to contemplate happily and exclusively anything that supports it. For one's beliefs are *to a point* (a point which varies with the person) within one's voluntary control. One can dwell imaginatively upon whatever supports them, keep one's attention

carefully off whatever clashes with them, and in this way reinforce the beliefs one chooses to 'cultivate'. If this, however, is
the policy that the 'duty to believe' doctrine is commending, then
it is a policy that conflicts harshly with a certain *other* policy that
many thoughtful people might hold to be far more urgently
obligatory. It is the policy of the impartial heeding of evidence
for *and* against one's beliefs, particularly evidence *against* them,
which one constantly tends to play down in importance. This is
so fruitful a policy that it would take very strong arguments indeed to displace it—arguments far stronger than any the theologian offers for his 'duty to believe'.[1] In any case, the theologian
stands to suffer if his opponents took leave also to abandon it: for
then they would be equally at liberty to claim *their* beliefs as
obligatory and to judge the Christian as not only intellectually in
error but also morally perverse. In other words, the adopting of
the policy of 'duty to believe' in a thorough-going way would
immediately lead to the utter frustrating of discussion; it would
make it impossible for *either* disputant to discover and admit that
his position was weaker than the other. The theologian would
have provided the means whereby his opponent could effectively
stop up his ears against the gospel he proclaimed to him, and do so
with a perfectly serene conscience.

7

Drawing together this discussion: I have not tried to ignore or
deny the very real value of present-day Christological thinking in
theology. If it is a distinctively *Christian* faith that is 'in search of
understanding', then the theologian who tries to understand it
ought to realize that Christianity is *about* the revelation of a
transcendent God within history: it is *about* the infinite becoming

[1] I owe certain of these points to Professor H. H. Price's paper 'Belief
and Will', Aristotelian Society Supplementary Volume XXVIII, 1954,
pp. 1 ff.

finite, the invisible becoming visible, the Word becoming flesh. Any theologian who does not see this is not likely to present a *Christian* theology, whatever else he may do.

It does not follow from this, however, that theologians have managed successfully to carry through the rigorous programme that I have been calling 'strict Christology'. It seems to me, rather, that few have yet made this attempt with real single-mindedness or in detail enough to constitute a 'crucial experiment' that could test their claims. The verdict here is 'not proven'; plus a suspicion that it is only by covert reference to the 'banned' metaphysical, speculative language that the Christologists' arguments actually move forward and obtain release from the prison of the finite and the immanent and the relative. But only if they *had* succeeded in that programme could we be meaningfully commanded to take the leap of faith in the Christian direction. As Professor A. N. Prior has well put it: if the believer's hypothesis is meaningless, the choice between it and a meaningful alternative cannot be a fifty-fifty gamble, nor even a hundred to one, but 'a hundred to nothing against belief'.[1]

The shape of my argument is therefore quite closely parallel to that of the chapters on 'encounters'. In these it was claimed that it might be reasonable to talk of our situation as 'ambiguous', since it is about just as plausible to interpret the 'sense of encounter' as a real meeting as to interpret it as the illusion of one. But the ambiguity vanishes if one or other of the alternatives can be shown as meaningless: for then it ceases to exist *as* an alternative.[2]

The Christologist cannot evade the linguistic problem (I went on to argue) by first admitting the breakdown in meaning within the language he uses, but then going on to say that it means something privately to the believer, or is still a vehicle used by God. These moves rely on untenable theories of meaning. And lastly, if statements about God have still not been exhibited as meaningful,

[1] *New Essays in Philosophical Theology*, p. 8.
[2] Cf. above, pp. 85 ff.

it is no help to preface them with moral imperatives to believe what they 'say'. Meaningless statements say nothing intelligible. But this is only one of the many difficulties about that muddled and unlovely doctrine which reduces all unbelief to sinful estrangement.

Assuming for the moment that there is no problem of *meaning* to worry us, we could say that the Christological theologian is logically entitled to reject appeals to criteria or features of his religion, in speaking of the ultimate choice between belief and unbelief. The leap of faith is not a ridiculous notion. What *can* be doubted is whether many Christians have thought through imaginatively what this view really implies—or have been given the chance to do so by their theological leaders. It means that statements that begin, 'I believe in Christ because . . .' can be completed only by some form of words drawn from within the content of Christianity itself, and thus not acceptable to the sceptic as backing for Christianity. Quite literally it implies that there is *nothing to choose between* Christianity and some of its alternatives. But the starkness of this is normally veiled by the preacher or theologian through his use of internal testimonies of Christianity to its own truth *as though* these were in fact independent testimony *from without*.

There seems no way of directly challenging this extraordinary position. The Christian theologian is, as I say, logically entitled to it. So is the exponent of any theology whatever, theologies fantastic as you please. They can all readily produce internal testimonies to their truth, and they can all deny that any other appeals are going to count, for or against. But I find myself unable to believe that any sane and serious Christian really holds his faith in this way. Assuming that his belief is centred on a Christology, he is far more likely to justify the place he gives to Jesus in his thought by reference to the total impression Jesus has made on him in his study of the New Testament. This view (which I have mentioned from time to time but not extensively discussed) would at least allow the discussion to go on, and to do so fruitfully. *Is* Jesus, we should ask, the sort of person who is worthy of the unconditional obedience the Christian yields him? And is the Christian's vision of Jesus based on a fair selection of what data we have about him, or does he have to avert his gaze from much that would *modify* the impact, and *qualify* the submission?

CHAPTER SIX
HISTORICITY AND RISK (1)

———

I

THERE is a great area of theological reasoning at which we have scarcely glanced so far: reasoning that is aimed not at singling out God directly or indirectly for *ostensive definition*, but at displaying him as the *explanation* of certain phenomena. The phenomena that he is held to explain may be restricted to particular historical events, notably miracles, or extended (say) to moral experience or even to the whole universe, which is said to demand an Author or First Cause. If the concept of God is indispensable to the explaining of these phenomena, then, however paradoxical it may seem to be, we cannot afford to scrap it. In this and the following chapter we shall sift through some recent arguments used by Christian writers attempting to interpret historical events in terms of the divine activity. Chapter Eight will discuss the relation of belief in God to moral experience: and Chapters Nine and Ten the 'Cosmological Argument' from the existence of a world to the 'Ground' of its existence. In none of these studies will anything like a comprehensive outline of current argumentation be attempted: in each I shall simply select for discussion certain treatments of those problems that seem to me both influential and logically interesting.

Two general points must be made about arguments to God from history. In the first place, there is the difficulty of understanding how exactly events in time could speak of a God of eternity. This problem has already vexed us in the preceding

91

chapter, and it will be the main concern of Chapters Nine and Ten. It can be said here simply that the problem is no *more* tractable in this context than it was in its Christological setting. If it is hard to see how talk about finites and temporals can be logically constructed into talk of infinites and eternals, it is just as hard to see how finite and temporal events can be 'explained' by reference to the infinite and eternal. The more devotionally adequate our conception of God is, the worse the problem becomes. As Professor H. A. Hodges has said, the conception of God

> is the conception of something essentially mysterious and *incommensurable with all objects of our experience*, and these are attributes which it is hard to see as contributing to an explanatory hypothesis intended to account for particular facts. Yet it is just this mysterious character which makes God really God, which gives the specifically religious quality to the concept of Him.[1]

Second, if God is being appealed to as the explanation of the particular course that history has actually taken, it must matter supremely whether or not we have reliable evidence about what that course was like. Cast doubt on the historicity of, say, some New Testament events, and the explanation required for them may be imperilled to the same degree. Or if we come to disbelieve certain narratives and retain belief in others, the *kind* of explanation demanded will be likely to vary with our alterations in historical confidence. Certainly, we could not say *in advance* of historical researches, '*Whatever* I find, God will still be required as the only explanation possible of the historical events.' That is to say, if we are to treat God as an explanatory hypothesis demanded by particular events, we must be prepared to withdraw the hypothesis, if our investigations show that the events happened rather differently from what we originally thought.

[1] 'What is to become of philosophical theology?' in *Contemporary British Philosophy*, ed. Prof. H. D. Lewis (London: Allen and Unwin, 1956), p. 229; my italics.

And yet, an extraordinary amount of contemporary theology is devoted to arguments that try to deny this obvious point, arguments that try to show that the hypothesis can remain unchallenged even if we become radically agnostic about the events it is supposed to be explaining. The influence and popularity of these arguments will, I think, justify the space given to discussion of them in the following pages.

Of course the arguments of actual theologians are more diverse and complex than simplified philosophical outlines can suggest. For instance, the theologian does not always think of us as starting from historically attested events and thence arguing our way to God. Theological presuppositions can often undergird those preliminary decisions about whether certain events did or did not happen in the past. And this complicates the whole problem.

Jesus being the Person he was, we are told, it is reasonable to accept the testimony of miracles told of him—with *less* evidential support than we should be right to demand in the case of other historical figures. Here is an argument *about* history and what we are to make of it, but involving appeal far *beyond* the data of history. The sceptic also uses such an argument if he says that *no* testimony could reasonably convince us that certain things occurred: it would always be more reasonable to distrust the testimony than accept the event. To which comes the obvious reply that the empiricist has less right than anyone else to lay down *a priori* what is and is not possible. In particular, the Christian may argue, one has no right to demand specially favoured attestation for any group of historical events. We have enough evidence of the broad historicity of the New Testament for faith to be a possibility. God does not compel us into slavish (and hence worthless) belief. But, on the same level of debate, his opponent may protest that the margin of historical probability in what the New Testament describes is so small (if it exists at all) as not to look like the signature of a loving God revealing himself graciously to man, but more like a God who torments him with uncertainty about whether or not a revelation has taken place in history.

And so it goes on. . . . Neither sceptic nor Christian can dodge those disputes on the periphery of historical research: both equally must be concerned with establishing valid ways of interpreting what data there are, of evaluating the different presuppositions that can swing the balance of judgement from belief to unbelief or back. Today, both are forced to agree on the one hand that the Scriptures are by no means historically infallible, and on the other, that there is no good reason to deny that a man called Jesus lived and taught. With those short-cuts blocked, the argument over historicity must be long and irreducibly complex. Indeed, our main quarrel in these chapters will be with theologians who fail to see how complex it is, and seek prematurely a secure resting-place for an imperturbable faith. The radical critics, we shall see, with their theological followers, are especially tempted to exploit certain important ambiguities in the notion of 'history', in order to hide the nakedness of the critical land. Alternatively, they are blunt in confessing how meagre the historical data are; but exhibit this not as catastrophe, but as triumph. God's chosen mode of revelation, they say, uses the limitations, the finitude and fragility, of human historical existence as its vehicle: precisely here is his condescending love in action. But, we shall have to ask, does not this approach run a serious risk of cutting off the very branch upon which the theologian is perched? For the less his historical data are to be trusted, the more uncertain it must be whether God *has* condescended. . . .

As a preface to our more detailed discussion of specific arguments, it may be useful to offer the merest outline of some phases of recent historical criticism.

The nineteenth- and early twentieth-century attempts to recover the 'biography' of Jesus, to strip off theological accretions, legendary embellishments, and so on, all unexpectedly collapsed. Renan, most memorably, aimed at 'rewriting it according to those canons of what is probable and intelligible in human

94

life'.[1] Harnack's *What is Christianity?* (1900) took the core of the Gospel to be (inoffensively) the fatherhood of God and the dignity of human life. Loisy and Guignebert attempted reconstructions from a radical critical standpoint.

These collapsed when Albert Schweitzer and others showed that the Gospels were mutilated, not restored, by removing the references to 'eschatology'—the dramatic interventions by God into history. If we are entitled to say anything about how Jesus saw his own vocation, it was not as gentle, Arcadian poet-preacher but as herald of imminent divine judgement. Historical critics became less and less sure that the Gospels (even Mark, the earliest) took pains over chronological sequence, that they provided the materials for a possible life-history of Jesus. The Gospel-writers were interested far more in the grouping of 'sayings', parables, similarly patterned miracle-stories to fill out the stylized 'kerygma', the form in which the earliest proclamations of the faith were couched. No probing behind the extant documents revealed any level at which the miraculous and prophetic 'accretions' had not yet appeared. There was, accordingly, nothing either rational or scientific in holding to the Jesus of the Liberal biographies.

'Form Criticism' argued, and still argues, that there is compelling evidence that the stories we have about Jesus were given their common literary patterns through their liturgical and apologetic employment in the life of the early Church. They are not straightforward pieces of reportage: if we see Jesus through them, it is Jesus as reflected in the mirror of Church life. He is not independently accessible to us in the way Renan and company supposed. We may have good reasons for trusting the interpretation of his life provided by the Gospel-writers, but little or no hope of confirming it by reference to his original actions and words.

Influential though Form Criticism is, not all scholars accept its scepticism about piercing the veil between early Church and historical Jesus. They differ over the thickness or flimsiness of that veil and over legitimate methods of probing it. Is it so thin

---

[1] Dean Church, reviewing Renan's *Vie de Jésus* (1863).

that the testimony of the New Testament to the empty tomb, the details of the resurrection appearances, may be trusted much as they stand? Or so thick that one can conclude only that after Jesus' death 'something happened'—something commensurate with the sudden transformation of the apostles' grief to infectious joy? We shall glance in a later part of this study at one method of reasoning back to the events, a method which assumes that the early Church altered its fund of memories of Jesus in a few discoverable directions that can be reversed in imagination and thus allow a good deal of penetration behind the veil. The disagreements that are, however, of greater interest to us are not those over what we *can* know about Jesus, but about how much we *need* to know before Christian faith is adequately supported.

2

Consider first some arguments of those Christians who believe we have little or no hope of access to 'the Jesus of history', and who yet insist that in some sense Christianity is tenable as a historical religion. Tillich denies that the Christian could live as if any day the postman might bring fatal tidings of some historical discovery that upset his verdict about Jesus. He denies also that the Christian *need* live at the mercy of the historian. We can understand very well the uneasiness of the view he rejects, especially since the 'peace of God' is one of the promised fruits of the Spirit: but it is altogether a different question whether this uneasiness can be avoided without loss of intellectual integrity; whether the Christian can fashion for himself an account of revelation, thoroughly 'historical', and yet allowing him to exclaim, as some do exclaim, that 'we are relieved of the intolerable burden of anxiety concerning historical researches into the detail of Jesus' existence'.[1] Conscious sophistry is not a fair accusation

[1] D. D. Williams, *Interpreting Theology, 1918–1952* (London: S.C.M., 1953), p. 105.

against these writers: but some devices by which anxiety is being stilled are logically most curious.

One of the commonest and most fashionable of these is the distinction (borrowed from the existentialists) between 'objective history' and 'personal grasp of meaning'. . . . It is one thing to recall detachedly what happened in the past: it is another thing to resolve to model one's behaviour on some pattern exemplified there, to take it as revealing unrealized possibilities of present and future experience. A scholar might devote his lifetime to historical detective-work upon the resurrection and fail ever to feel its imaginative and moral impact, to meditate or pray over it, or ever to understand why one should wish to write music about it like the music Bach wrote to the words '*Et resurrexit* . . .'

No historical religion is exclusively or even predominantly interested in the objective-historical, the brutely factual. The 'existential-historical', the second alternative, is its major concern. Even of historical study *in general*, not only within a religion, it may be said that the primary quest is always for the revelation of alternative *modes of human existence*, not the accumulation of inventories of facts. The archaeologist is no exception: his fragments of pottery, charred rubble, coins, and crumbled dykes are taken as clues to a pattern of living, not extant, but (because *human*) of present 'human interest'. Approaching from the other side; if one shows that some mode of existence is a human possibility, one may have done more to establish its 'existential-historicity' than if one had proved by objective-historical research that people *did* live that way at one particular point of time in the past. Conversely: to linger indefinitely over the establishing of objective history can be a way of evading the existential (practical, moral) demands of the way of life in question.

Reinhold Niebuhr works this distinction hard, when he says of the Cross and resurrection, 'It is the revelatory depth of the fact which is the primary concern of faith', *not* the confirming of it as an event of the past 'through specific historical details'.[1]

[1] *Faith and History* (London: Nisbet, 1949), p. 167.

97

Scientific detachment is not the attitude in which the New Testament should be investigated. 'The revelatory power of this whole story, drama, event, and person requires that it be viewed not as a spectator might view an ordinary drama.'[1] It requires to be 'apprehended by man in the total unity of his personality and not merely by his reason'.[2] For Niebuhr there is something blasphemous in the very search for confirmation of the New Testament claims for Christ. Only people who are culpably lacking in faith pry after miracles certified as objective history, in order to work up conviction. In short, 'faith's apprehension of the significance of the story' matters far more than the confirming of the events as ancient history, sheerly past and done with.[3]

If now the Gospel-writers, having 'apprehended the significance' of the resurrection, yet altered the factual details in writing of it; if they told of an empty tomb instead of the objective-factual 'experience of communion' with Jesus, which was the *hard* fact—we have, Niebuhr concludes, no cause for alarm. He is convinced that the attitudes of spectator or reporter are not appropriate to the 'saving events': the Gospel-writers cannot be censured for not assuming these attitudes. Far from accusing them of making their case for the resurrection stronger than they were entitled to, Niebuhr suggests instead that 'the sense of the [revelatory] dimension of the story influences the telling of the narrative'.[4] We do not have objective history in our Gospels: but then objective history is neither the only nor the most important sort of history. 'The story of this triumph over death is thus shrouded in a mystery which places it in a different order of history than the story of the crucifixion.'[5] A different order from the objective-historical crucifixion; but still *history*. The real miracle is not to be searched for in the obscure lumber-rooms of objective history. It lies before our eyes: the miracle of belief in the resurrection, without which the Church would not exist.[6] In the next paragraph this becomes—'[the Church] is

---

[1] *Faith and History* (London: Nisbet, 1949), p. 160. [2] *Ibid., loc. cit.*
[3] *Ibid.,* p. 166. [4] *Ibid., loc. cit.* [5] *Loc. cit.* [6] *Ibid.,* p. 167.

founded in the miracle of the recognition of the true Christ in the resurrection'.

Now for some comments on this strange piece of argumentation.

Nothing here is strictly self-contradictory. Granting that there might be good reasons for taking the resurrection-accounts as Neibuhr takes them, as an authentic communion with the risen Christ, embellished (piously) with non-objective 'detail'; we should be committed to an important part of the Christian claim. But a rather serious snag is that we have been given no independent evidence for the trustworthiness of *taking* the accounts in this way. All the early evidence is in these same documents. Putting it generously, Niebuhr has yet to show us that we are justified in believing that the New Testament writers interpreted whatever events there were along *sound* lines, and did not distort or warp them. This trustworthiness is assumed and not argued for, when they are said to have apprehended the 'revelatory significance' of the events. Second, Niebuhr does not believe it is necessary to ask whether the sense of communion with the risen Christ could have been infallible and self-authenticating, as he again seems to assume. Yet it by no means follows from the fact that someone has a sense 'as of personal encounter' that there stands over against him some real person. This, we saw earlier, was a serious difficulty in arguing from experiences of *I–Thou* encounter to God. Genuine personal relations certainly do have an immediacy, a directness, and uniqueness; but this sense of immediacy is not self-authenticating, cannot infallibly answer the questions, 'Is there a person here or not? Is there someone here with whom I *can* enter on personal relations?' But if you are confronted with a human form, human facial expression, gestures, a voice responsive in conversation (and the 'detailed' resurrection-narratives provide all these with respect to the risen Christ), then the possibilities of illusion, hallucination, and the rest are enormously diminished. They are reduced to vanishing-point when *all* the features present in a normal meeting with a person are present also in the case in question.

99

To see this is to see what a dubious exchange Niebuhr is offering. We are to deny objective historicity to the resurrection stories, and trust instead to a sense of contact with Jesus after death, which seems at least as fallible as any documentary account about the rolling away of a stone or angels at the tomb. Niebuhr seems unconscious of having missed any steps in the argument, when he goes on to speak, not of the Christian *conviction* about the risen Jesus, nor about a *sense* of encounter, but (as if all alternatives had been ruled out) of 'this *triumph*', which no one ought on pain of blasphemy to try to confirm. If we still say that the resurrection, though not accessible to objective-historical research, belongs nevertheless to 'a different order of history', are we saying any more than that some people, past and present, have a sense *as of* the presence of Christ? If we read more into Niebuhr's words, as he himself intends we should, are we logically *entitled* to do so? In particular, we can no longer bring forward the objective historicity of Christ's resurrection as the *justification* of the otherwise rash assertion that all these senses of presence have been and are of the same person, identical with Jesus of Nazareth. And that appeal to objectivity here has undoubtedly been the supreme traditional defence against possibilities of imaginative illusion.

We are offered not only an event in 'a different order of history', but also a '*miracle* of a different order'—the miracle of belief in the resurrection. What sort of miracle could this be? Miraculous, because founded on tenuous evidence? But we should certainly not want to attribute to the God of Christianity the miraculous implanting of some belief, unless we knew that that belief was true. If it were false or highly dubious, we should perhaps marvel at the stubbornness with which people continued to believe it, but hardly attribute its persistence to a God of truth and wisdom. Yet, in the present case, how *can* we independently confirm the truth of the belief in the resurrection, or show it to be false?

To put the problem in a different way:

'What was the miracle?'

'The miracle was that tenacious refusal to believe death had put an end to Jesus.'

'Miracle? Why don't you simply call it an inexplicable or just surprising belief: for the history of belief in the resurrection *may* be the history of a stubborn illusion. "Miracle" strongly suggests that this belief was divinely implanted in man and, since God does not deceive, must be true.'

'Exactly: it certainly is true.'

'But unless you have evidence inaccessible to other believers, you are in no position to say with authority: This is miracle, not illusion; or that people had little solid evidence to go on, but, thanks to God, they were right in their beliefs. Besides, to call belief in the resurrection "the real miracle" suggests that somehow, because this real miracle has occurred, we have better grounds for belief than if it had not occurred: the miracle is itself supplementary evidence for the resurrection. But this would be so only if the "miracle" of belief could be shown independently to emanate from God (whatever such a demonstration would be like). That it was a *true* belief might count in favour of divine origin: but even this, I've insisted, cannot be shown apart from that very same evidence on which the belief is based. All we have is the evidence of the early Church in the New Testament: to call belief *upon* that evidence "miraculous", is to beg the crucial question of its reliability, not to make belief more reasonable, or more plausible, or even more wonderful.'

Before leaving Niebuhr, more must be said about the issue with which this discussion commenced, the deflection of scrutiny from objective history to its existential meaning. One thing can be stated confidently: before we can say, 'It is the revelatory depth of the fact that is the primary concern of faith', we must already be sure that there *is* a fact (objective-historically), and that it *has* revelatory depth. Attempts at confirming the fact are blasphemous only if for quite other reasons we could say, Jesus is undoubtedly Son of God. But if we *were* able to say that, our need for confirmation (for the resurrection or any other event in his life) would be very much less! As it stands, we cannot say anything of the kind, least of all if we base belief in the resurrection upon any illusion-prone 'sense of communion'. Above all, it cannot be reprehensible for faith not to be sure of itself, if that faith is dubiously supported.[1] Niebuhr himself presumably wishes to retain the words by which to say exactly this about non-Christian faiths—that they are not as well founded as his own. Nothing could be odder than to censure anxiety about the basis of faith in the very course of investigating whether that faith is or is not well based. And nothing could better show up the quixotic effects of existentialist and quasi-existentialist approaches to historicity.

It would be altogether different if Niebuhr saw Christianity as no more or less than a manner of living, a moral and social code, an imaginative 'slant' on the world like that of a poet or a novelist. Then, the exchange of objective history for existential would be no real loss at all. Provided that we had a blue print of that way of life, it would be of no importance whether that blue print took the form of parable, fable, legend, or the narration of what also happened to be objectively historical. But Niebuhr constantly speaks as if Christianity were much more than this. The resurrection is not just a *good idea* with valuable moral implications. It does not simply spotlight existing human possibilities, but claims to have brought *new* possibilities, of being reconciled to God, of being resurrected with Jesus, and so on; possibilities that are not open if the resurrection never took place. In short, to mishandle the distinction between the objective and existential levels of history can easily obscure that vital difference between (i) alternative ways of life, which are equally well delineated by fiction as by narration of fact, and (ii) claims like the Christian claim that, but for certain events of the past, the present possibilities would be other than they are. Questions of objective history thus cannot be smuggled out of the way by extolling the importance of the 'significance for life' of the doctrines concerned. The appeal to

[1] Compare Chapter Five above, pp. 84 ff.

significance cannot properly displace the anxiety and risk attending historical research into New Testament origins. Or, if it can, Niebuhr has not shown how.

3

Let us try again. Quite recently, F. Gogarten, the Göttingen theologian, published a work called *Demythologizing and History*.[1] This is an explicit attempt, in brief compass, to justify the most daring flight from the objective-historical, while insisting with all possible emphasis that his own theology is 'historical' through and through. It is a stridently polemical work, very relevant to our present study, since a good deal of his argumentation is directed against just the sort of points I have been making in answer to Niebuhr.

Gogarten starts by saying in effect: Try taking the common-sensical, objective-historical line if you want to. See where it leads you. See, in fact, if it does not lead you into far worse nonsense than you accuse the existentialist historian of perpetrating. Suppose your New Testament events were confirmed by every objective test known to historical science. What then? Would your Christianity be proved true? Far from it. For to draw *religious* conclusions from the objective-historical events is to do much more than to acknowledge that this man received his sight and that man came to life again. It is to interpret the events as being related in some important way to the unconditioned, eternal, infinite being that is God: to call them manifestations of his power, his love, and so on. This is no longer purely historical talk: the events as religious revelation are *not* 'historically comprehensible'.[2] The nonsense appears in the efforts made to reconcile these demands—the events are *in* history, but somehow or other point

[1] Stuttgart: 1953: London: S.C.M., 1955.
[2] For the argument which I am paraphrasing, see Gogarten, *op. cit.*, pp. 39 ff.

beyond history, are *in* space and time, and yet tell us of a being who is in neither. Can the orthodox believer work out these problems with any *less* breakdown in logic than can be laid at the door of existentialist historians? Very probably not. Here Gogarten and I are in substantial agreement.

But here too, alas, our agreement ends. Gogarten proceeds to argue that one can be as sceptical about metaphysics as one likes and interpret revelation in its entirety as an 'historical' phenomenon, provided one does not restrict 'history' to sheer, objective past events. We are reminded again of the Niebuhr arguments when Gogarten writes, 'the actual historical character . . . of the events recorded in the New Testament, is not to be sought in the "objective" and historically [*objective*-historically] ascertainable fact of their having taken place, but in the . . . proclamation and witness that in the events of this history God turns with grace towards mankind. . . .' [1] Obviously too the same primary *objection* to Niebuhr applies equally to Gogarten. Events of history have to be realized existentially, if they are to be more to us than brute facts about the past. But to be realized existentially, they must first be facts. Prayer to a living Jesus today is a possibility only if Jesus did rise in the first century A.D.

Look once more at the sentence I quoted. It begins by turning away from the task of confirming objectively that there *were* such events as the New Testament describes. Then, more approvingly, it speaks of the 'proclamation and witness that in the events of this history God turns . . .'. In what events? Why, the objective-historical events whose reality is surely being assumed, despite all the disclaimers. But we have no business assuming it, *whatever* the historical critics say, nor to deny that their verdict might falsify certain crucial claims, or might back them up. Least of all can we afford to look forward to the day when 'such chimeras and phantasmagorias as "objective-factualness" and "objectively real events" will quite automatically disappear'. [2]

The reader will not be surprised to find that, because of Go-

[1] Gogarten, *op. cit.*, pp. 37 f.   [2] *Ibid.*, p. 89.

garten's insistence that the significance of the events matters more than their occurrence or non-occurrence, several quite definite questions of *objective* historicity are either begged or shunned. For example, he tells us to approach miracle with neither the closed mind of scepticism nor the too-open mind of superstition, but simply ask of a miracle its significance as Word of God:[1] we must ask what can be learned here about God's redeeming activity. It would seem, however, to follow that an entirely fictional miracle-story, whose implications were consistent at all points with the divine will, should be accepted as of equal status and authority with any New Testament miracle—a conclusion from which, presumably, Gogarten would vigorously recoil, if he could be brought to face this issue squarely. He contents himself with ruling out one alternative (confirmation of miracle through objective-historical research), as a serious case of 'objectifying' God and God's Word, and so denying him.[2] This, of course, is closely parallel to Niebuhr's charges of blasphemy against 'blameworthy' scepticism. It is hard to see any real strength in Gogarten's equation of 'objectifying God' and pursuing historical research into the occurrence of miracles. Grant that God confronts man as a subject, a *Thou*, not as an object. It is quite compatible with this that he should choose certain events in the world through which to manifest himself. There are difficulties enough in understanding how the eternal could break into time; but to speak of God as personal and to speak of him acting through events does not seem to me to involve a contradiction in terms. On these assumptions, we should know what God was revealing only by discovering (perhaps with difficulty) what exactly these events had been like. We should certainly miss the revelation if we lost track of the events. (Though we might still miss it if we noticed only the events, but failed to grasp their meaning.) Taking their objective historicity utterly seriously, would, on this view, be no violation of God's personal being: quite the reverse.

Of these events, Christians have maintained, the Cross and

[1] Gogarten, *op. cit.*, pp. 86 ff. [2] *Ibid.*, p. 87.

resurrection are the most revealing of all. Because these things happened, we are entitled to speak of God's love and forgiveness. Compare, however, Gogarten. The Cross indeed 'has its origin in time in the historical occurrence of the crucifixion of Jesus of Nazareth; but one would be setting one's reliance upon the world . . . if one were to seek in this for the trustworthiness of the contents of the tradition. *The tradition must carry within itself and nowhere else the trustworthiness which is here being enquired for.*'[1] Somehow in the very fact of the proclamation of the Gospel the Christian is to find his confirmation; and not in the well-foundedness of what is proclaimed.

'The tradition must carry within itself . . .' What sort of 'must' is this? 'Must', if there is to be no risk of historical falsification: 'must', in order to keep anxiety at bay? Once again we have to discriminate; between the truth that it is only in hearing *about* the Cross or resurrection that I can come to realize what significance it may have for my life; and the error that this testimony itself is self-certifying, that it ought not to be challenged as to its sound or flimsy base in objective history.

The word which, more than any other, comes to one's lips in reading both Niebuhr and Gogarten is 'subjectivism'. It is a subjectivism of the most thorough-going kind. Instead of the verification of the original events, we are told that what matters is the impact of *talk* about the events. Instead of objective resurrection appearances, we have to be content with a sense of communion in believers. But Gogarten, and his master Bultmann, deny this charge of subjectivism with an elaborate and far-reaching argument. In their own language, the Christian's understanding is 'transformed into an extremely subjectivistic phenomenon of consciousness which as such has no bearing on reality . . .' *only if* it is 'transposed into the subject–object pattern'.[2] What does this mean? We can best approach it by glancing back at a point made earlier in this chapter. It is claimed that men are not able to contemplate history with complete detachment, as one

[1] Gogarten, *op. cit.*, p. 77, my italics.   [2] *Ibid.*, p. 55.

regards a specimen on a dissecting-table; you the subject, it the object. Since all history is human history, what we find there is the world, not as it is in itself, but as it looks through the eyes of men who are involved in all sorts of ways with it. We do not know what man in the abstract would be like. We know only particular men and women in particular historical contexts. We have no idea what the world would look like to beings without our needs, tasks, and capacities. We cannot speak properly here either of 'isolated subjects' or of 'isolated objects'. If one called Gogarten's interpretation '*subjectivist*', one would be implying that it could be contrasted with a purely '*objectivist*' interpretation in which the subject is reduced to a neutral, detached, anonymous observer. But this has been ruled out as impossible.

Two points of criticism, however, suggest themselves. (i) The argument owes much to the fashionable existentialist horror of a mechanized civilization. It sees clearly, but exaggerates, the pressures today tending to reduce people to mere machine-operators. themselves manipulated by social scientists, as 'de-personalized' human automata. The operator's relation to his machine is *par excellence* a detached subject–object relation; and (because of this fear of lost personality) that relation itself, whenever it occurs, comes to be deprecated as degrading. But it is clearly not the same thing (*a*) to draw attention to the dangers of the subject–object relation *dominating* human life—a nightmare indeed; and (*b*) ruling it out as improper in every context. The special sciences may provide highly important data for the morally serious man: the psychological, sociological, criminological sciences do so: why not the historical? In all these no philosophical *fiat* can reasonably eliminate the need for subject–object relations; for objectivity.

Gogarten further claims [1] that even within science 'the subject–object scheme of thought' has been 'rendered untenable'. And indeed there are experimental situations in which no observation of atomic particles is possible without interfering with these by the very act of observation itself. But the sole conclusion from

[1] Gogarten, *op. cit.*, p. 51.

such cases, interpreted in this way, is that ideal experimental conditions are practically impossible, *not* that a certain attitude and relation to the subject-matter of study is untenable.

(ii) How much truth is there in the additional claims, first that man is 'responsible for the form of the world'[1]: he is not the passive spectator of 'given' events, but to a large extent makes them what they are by seeing them in the light of his purposes, ideals, imperfections, and so on: and that, second, the search for the absolutely given datum of objective history is simply not worth attempting—and, besides, impossible?

That there *is* truth here cannot be denied. Man's view of the world can safely be said to be very different from an eagle's or a rabbit's. What the impressionist 'sees' is not the same tree (to exaggerate only very slightly) as the cubist who stands at his side. The 'same' landscape (say, a valley with a river) is very different to the bridge-constructing engineer and the native revisiting the scene of his childhood. And doubtless this is true of past as well as present events. Nevertheless, it is not nonsense to speak of the *common* tree or the *common* landscape. Cut down the tree, or dam up the river, and *all* the existentially involved painters, engineers, and natives will have a radically altered view. We have not been forced to deny a limit to creativity, a core of hard fact. Why, similarly, should not the historian be seen as building *his* interpretation upon often meagre but quite indispensable cores of objective factuality?

There are limits, in other words, to the malleability of events under imagination or 'interpretation'. Faces in the fire can be seen with *nearly* limitless variety; a poem may bear a *fair number* of reasonable optional interpretations, though not any and every interpretation; a penny may be seen as circle or ellipse, but not as a cone or a cube. So with historical investigations. A scrutiny of each case is necessary before a decision can be made about the reasonableness of any particular interpretation based upon available knowledge.

[1] Gogarten, *op. cit.*, pp. 48 ff.

Equally vital is the further question: 'Does my knowledge of the "event" give me enough information to back up an interpretation of *any* kind? Or is scepticism the only sensible response?' We might ask, 'What crossed the path just now, ahead of us in the shadows? A mouse? a ferret? a low-flying blackbird?' We cannot tell; it was too quick, unexpected, far away.

Thus man is neither the witness of a succession of ready-made events complete with their 'meanings', nor does he fashion the world by his own creativity. Both these exaggerations are equally fatal to a sound philosophy of history.

4

While the origin of these views on historicity is continental, their influence is increasingly strong in British theological writing. They cannot simply be dismissed, therefore, as a remote curiosity of thought, an aberration (uncongenial to the Anglo-Saxon mind) from concreteness and empiricism. The problem of how to maintain a historical religion on what little pure history the biblical critics have left us has been felt so persistently embarrassing, that the Heidegger–Bultmann 'solution' is winning many converts. The unhappy effect of this can perhaps best be seen in a work that is largely a study of Bultmann, and Heidegger—John Macquarrie's *An Existentialist Theology*. Dr Macquarrie has a good stock of straightforward commonsense. With what thankfulness one reads, 'There could only be saving events if there had been certain objective events.'[1] We have touched down in the sanity of objective history. Only temporarily, however. The Bultmann influence prompts Macquarrie to say *also* that, were the New Testament events thoroughly confirmed by the historian, that would not make much difference for religious faith, 'and frankly, it would be intolerable if it did. For then not only the theologian but the ordinary Christian believer would be at the mercy of the

[1] *An Existentialist Theology* (London: S.C.M., 1955), p. 170.

historian'.[1] But if my arguments in the present chapter have shown anything at all they have shown that no amount of subtlety can provide historicity without the *risks* of historicity. Moreover, Macquarrie believes that the primary confirmation of the 'fact' of the resurrection lies to hand in the 'present possibility' offered by Christ through the proclamation of the Word. It is from *this* that 'we infer that something did once happen . . . '. What it was is 'a matter for academic speculation only'.[2] Again, how can it be only academic? If any of these theologians had sat down to consider in turn possible alternative explanations of the believer's experience, his senses of communion, his moral seriousness, reckoning especially with the Freudian analysis in its most challenging forms; and if then he reasonably concluded that the Christian interpretation was the most plausible one, the doubter (convinced or not) could at least have no complaints over the theologian's thoroughness. But this is *not* what we find. We find a terminology calculated to turn aside all such questions about valid and invalid interpretation, to rule them out as psychological irrelevancies. The present inquiry, we are told, is theology, irreducibly such. Yet once more, psychology surely cannot be ruled out as irrelevant here. For what Macquarrie and company are claiming is that from a consideration of the way the world looks to Christians today, the way they feel, the possibilities of life open to them, one and only one interpretation is valid: that the resurrection of Jesus occurred. Alternative explanations are not worth attempting.

Suppose, lastly, that the Christian explanation did seem the most reasonable one—with only a small margin over, say, the Freudian account. Then suppose further that we consulted the historian who was able to provide confirmation of the actual occurrence of the events to which our analysis of the believer's experience seemed, all in all, to point. Would we not have every reason to rejoice in this extraordinary corroboration? The theologian could not deny it—if he were not a captive to existentialist

[1] Macquarrie, *loc. cit.*   [2] *Ibid.*, pp. 188 f.

confusions. In the light of this, how unrealistic is Macquarrie's disclaimer that 'attempts . . . to prove that the tomb was empty . . . are simply beside the point, for in its character as saving event the resurrection is to be understood existentially'.[1]

In conclusion, if we accept Gogarten's either/or; *either* the orthodox stress on objective historicity, *or* the existentialists' account, then *both* ways seem equally blocked; the first for roughly the reasons Gogarten mentions, and the second for the reasons adduced in our present discussion. Of course, there may be other, unnoticed, options, among them (though the theologian so often forgets it) a reluctant suspension of belief. Better that perhaps than the conversion of a disappointingly negative biblical criticism into an obscurantist mock-triumph.

[1] Macquarrie, p. 188.

CHAPTER SEVEN

HISTORICITY AND RISK (2)

———————

I

ONE English theologian whose apologetic works are widely
read is Professor Alan Richardson.[1] Perhaps equally influential is the *Theological Word Book of the Bible*, which he edited,
and to which he contributed several of the main articles. The
problem of historicity is prominent in these works, and his treatment of it deserves serious discussion here. We shall confine our
attention in this chapter almost entirely to Professor Richardson's
approach, rather than skim superficially over a plurality of
theories. We shall find that several of the ideas already discussed
reappear in this writer (a further testimony to their importance in
contemporary British thought), but Richardson adds original
arguments at many points and provides a particularly interesting
account of miracles.

In his book *Christian Apologetics* we meet the same paradox as
in Macquarrie's *An Existentialist Theology*. First, the Christian
faith 'is bound up with certain happenings in the past, and if these
happenings could be shown never to have occurred, or to have
been quite different from the biblical-Christian account of them,
then the whole edifice of Christian faith, life and worship would
be found to have been built on sand'.[2] It would surely seem to
follow that historical criticism could conceivably falsify belief.
But the reader will be conditioned by this stage against bewilder-

———

[1] See especially his *Christian Apologetics* (London: S.C.M., 1947).
[2] *Christian Apologetics*, p. 91.

ment, when he further learns that the Christian 'well knows that the question of the historicity of the miracles or of the Gospel record in general is not settled in the field of historical and critical research'.[1]

Richardson's defence of the paradox takes the following form. History involves selection: *this* is told, *that* is ignored. We bring to the facts a principle by which the selection is made. We bring a personal 'standpoint', a cast of mind, to which some historical explanations will make sense, others not. A person with one standpoint may well refuse to admit the historicity of something which another will swear by—on the same objective evidence. Yet without *some* standpoint, some 'faith-principle' as Richardson calls it, no history can be written at all. The most adequate 'faith-principle' will be the one that makes the greatest amount of sense out of the highest proportion of data. Hence, we do not first work out what took place and what did not take place, and *then* work out the significance of what did happen. There are not two operations: only one, in which data and significance are simultaneously discovered through applying a fruitful 'faith-principle' to the historical situation. On these assumptions, it should not surprise us if 'once the Christian meaning of the facts is denied, the facts themselves begin to disappear into the mists of doubt and vagueness'.[2]

Historicity is being seen by Richardson not primarily as involving *correspondence* with fact, but above all the *coherence* of the data in patterns, webs of significance. A wrong faith-principle obscures the pattern: the right one throws it into relief. Correspondence is not, however, *entirely* superseded. The true account will in fact correspond with what happened in the past, but 'since we can never know directly the facts which happened, correspondence is for us no criterion of objectivity at all'. [3] This is quite crucial to Richardson's whole position, as we shall see. At the moment, one comment may be made on the last-quoted sentence. There is truth in what it says, but it is stated far too strongly. It

[1] *Christian Apologetics*, p. 174.　　[2] *Ibid.*, p. 105.　　[3] *Ibid.*, p. 147.

seems to deny that a distinction can be made between (i) the evidence we have for the historicity of an event, and (ii) what we know about the relations between that event and others alleged to have occurred about the same time. We may know very well *that* an event happened, but be unable to integrate it into any coherent pattern at all: we should call it an anomaly, a candidate for future explanation; but we should not for that reason dismiss the good evidence we have of its actual *occurrence*.

Suppose, for example, I made a set of ten experiments in a laboratory yesterday morning. I have had no time as yet to work over the ten instrument-readings which they yielded. *Perhaps* they will 'cohere' beautifully in some pattern, as terms in a series; they may produce a neat curve if I represent them on a graph. I do not as yet know. But this does not reduce my confidence that I *have* the readings and that they are accurate. Discovering the series or the curve would boost my confidence that no slips, joltings, changes in conditions, had brought error into the experiment. Supposing the original data remained for many years untouched along with other figures in a notebook: to discover *then* that they showed a 'significant' pattern would be of still greater confirming value, reducing enormously the chance that they recorded, say, a list of random numbers, and not the results of an experiment; although by itself the coherence test might not prove enough to warrant sound inferences about the exact nature of the experiment from which they emanated.

Cases could be imagined in which discovery of very tight coherences might not confirm but *shake* belief in historicity. To extend the laboratory example: if I suspected that a set of figures had not in fact been properly arrived at by experiment, but instead had been 'cooked' by a lazy assistant, my suspicion would be deepened when I found that they were terms in a simple mathematical progression which my assistant had recently encountered in other connections.

Summing this up. We are not entitled to argue to historicity from a high degree of coherence considered by itself. In some cases such coherence as appears will reinforce our confidence about the data themselves: in others, it will be too good to be true. In others again (nearer the New Testament set of problems), it will be impossible or next to impossible to discover how much the original facts were 'adjusted' by their first reporters into nearest conformity with the pattern they sought to bring out in them and at which the facts indeed may have hinted. At any rate, there can be no short-cuts that avoid the weighing up of these options in each situation. And if coherence is not the adequate test Richardson maintains it to be, there is nothing for it but once again to take seriously the historical critics' attempts to keep *as separate as possible* the questions of event and significance.

Not only is the role of objective history minimized in *Christian Apologetics*, but the emphases on coherence and the search for a suitable faith-principle make the establishment of the New Testament events-and-significance seem a much easier task than it can really be.

> That perspective from which we see most clearly all the facts, without having to explain any of them away, will be a relatively true perspective. Christians believe that the perspective of biblical faith enables us to see very clearly and without distortion the biblical facts as they really are: they see the facts clearly because they see their true meaning. On the other hand, when once the Christian meaning of the facts is denied, the facts themselves begin to disappear . . .[1]

(i) An important question is begged in the first sentence. If we accept as the best perspective the one which allows us to see all the facts and explain none away, we are already assuming that none of the alleged 'facts' *ought* to be explained away, that the records are in the main trustworthy. A 'conservative' biblical critic would be able to say that, but not a radical critic. But to admit this is to see that the historical quest cannot be reduced to the quest for the coherence-bringing perspective.

[1] *Christian Apologetics*, p. 105.

(ii) The next sentence claims that the biblical perspective gives a clear, undistorted view of the 'biblical facts as they really are'. Does this advance the argument for Christian belief? It can only mean that once we grant the biblical presuppositions, the biblical account *coheres*. Which may be so; but cannot settle the question of its *truth or falsity*. A poem, a novel, a fugue, may all be coherent in their various ways: nothing follows as to whether the poet or novelist recorded actual past events in their works. And *musical* coherence is quite plainly unrelated to any reporting of events.

(iii) Christians 'see the facts clearly because they see their true meaning'. Maybe: but Richardson has not ruled out the possibility that Christians merely see *what the facts would have to be*, in order to bear the Christian interpretation. To see *this* is not the same as being persuaded that the facts were so.

(iv) In the light of these comments, the final sentence quoted comes to have a double edge to it. Deny the Christian 'meaning of the facts' and 'the facts themselves begin to disappear'. The doubter could take this as an admission of what I have said about (iii) above; re-emphasizing the extreme difficulty of settling what the facts were, as distinct from settling what they would have to be, in order to bear the meaning the Christian desires. Taking it this way, the doubter could only agree: but he would deny that in this group of arguments Richardson had achieved what he set out to achieve.

Going further; the notion of 'perspective', separable and distinguishable, able to be labelled 'biblical', 'naturalistic', and so on, can carry certain misleading suggestions. Although I approach the New Testament with a most sympathetic mind, my believing perspective may gradually and imperceptibly change to uncertainty and agnosticism through a great many intermediate positions, as I come to realize, say, the unanswered problems of meaning in religious concepts, the strength of psycho-analytic accounts of religious experience, and the tenuousness of historical evidence on which the religious system is raised. What the historical critic says is always relevant to the assessing of my overall position, whether this fact brings anxiety or not. Equally, if I interpret the New Testament on the principle that all the miraculous elements are free-fantasies on the (non-miraculous) life of a remarkable man, I should be intellectually dishonest, if I did not modify this perspective when I found that sometimes the New Testament authors neglected clear and easy opportunities of adding to the supernatural splendour of their writings. The epileptic boy in Mark's Gospel became 'as one dead; insomuch that many said, He is dead'. If the chosen perspective were sound, why on earth did not Mark take a hint from the majority of the eyewitnesses, and alter 'as dead' to 'dead'?[1] If the language of 'faith-principle' or 'perspective' is retained, then it must be stressed that adopting such a principle can be only a tentative venture, never finally confirmed while historical and theological research and discussion continue, giving no inviolate platform above the ebb and flow of controversy. The principle may (as Richardson insists) be brought *to* history, and may not be found there: nonetheless, it may have to be *corrected*, perhaps discarded, in obedience to what we do find in history.

As we have already noticed, there are many places in *Christian Apologetics* where Richardson means by a Christian faith-principle something more positive than this cast of mind: he takes it not merely as the readiness to heed the New Testament sympathetically, the refusal to write off its miracles *a priori* as absurd, but he takes it as being prepared to *accept its authority* about what it proclaims.

Belief in the historicity of the Gospel miracles does not come by means of any 'scientific' and 'objective' examination of the evidence: it comes when we decide to accept the testimony of the apostles concerning the things which they saw with their eyes and . . . handled concerning the Word of Life.[2]

[1] Mark 9, 26. On this point of criticism, see W. Manson, *Jesus the Messiah.* (London: Hodder and Stoughton, 1943), p. 46.

[2] *Christian Apologetics*, p. 172.

In taking up a pro-Christian perspective in *this* sense, of course, we have nothing to fear from critic or philosopher. But what has happened is that the conclusions which an apologetic struggles finally to reach have been pushed up into its initial *presuppositions*. One will now, for instance, have no difficulty in accepting the resurrection; not because sound evidence for it has been adduced, but only because one's study has been *prefaced* by an acceptance of the reliability of the disputed records.

A principle of interpretation, then, may be either an attitude of mind brought to an inquiry or it may include a set of more specific suppositions; or it may be located somewhere in the scale between these two poles. In general we may conclude that as historical vulnerability decreases, so too decreases the importance of the conclusions we can reach; and *vice versa*. The more *content* we give to our presuppositions, the more weight of justification must fall upon those presuppositions themselves. And we have seen above how difficult that justification is, where 'coherence' is the principal test employed.

2

The most acute historical problems of all have constantly centred upon the New Testament miracles. It has been to defend or reject those that believers and unbelievers alike have most clamantly invoked their rival 'perspectives', their notions of what is possible and impossible, what likely and unlikely, in the light of all that they independently know about the sort of world we live in. In his discussion of miracle, Professor Richardson wants, reasonably enough, to do justice both to our twentieth-century scientific knowledge of the world, and to that biblical faith-principle which he is anxious to maintain.[1] The principal question we shall put to him is, '*Can* these two aims be achieved together, harmoniously, as he believes they can?'

[1] See the books already quoted, and also the same author's *The Miracle Stories of the Gospels* (London: S.C.M., 1941).

What, first of all, is meant by 'miracle'? A two-fold definition is offered. (i) Miracles are not contrary to nature, but only contrary to what we *know* about nature. ' "Science" as such can have no objection to the conception of miracle as it is understood in traditional theology; for miracle is merely that which occurs according to the operation of those laws of nature which are as yet unknown to us.' [1]

(ii) 'The miraculous is that which arouses in us the feeling of wonder, of awe and even of humility in its presence.' [2] In this sense, the whole (law-obeying) universe may be called miraculous by anyone who finds it awe-inspiring. Adding together the two parts of the definition, we conclude that a miracle is an anomalous event that arouses awe. Anomalous, not because no explanation of it is theoretically possible in terms of natural law, but through our present ignorance of the laws involved. Awe-inspiring—but again, for all we know, law-abiding also. This definition clearly cannot offend the twentieth-century mind; but can it really cover all that the *New Testament* required of the concept of miracle? More, surely, is meant by Christ's 'signs' and 'wonders' than the performance of (at the time) unexplained events, which aroused awe in the spectators.

And indeed we find Richardson ceasing to speak of mere anomalies and speaking instead of the 'Gospel miracles', which 'were not the result of the operation of any force which the physical sciences can measure or describe'.[3] That the sciences *could* account for them could be believed only by someone who made the (philosophical) assumption that 'the only forces in the universe are those which physical science can measure'.[4] Now, our definition tells us that a miracle of today (in sense (i)) could cease to be miraculous tomorrow, if we found an explanation of it in terms of natural law. But today it is unexplained, miraculous. It would not be made any *more* miraculous by predicting that no such explanatory law would ever be found. That prediction, if taken seriously, would simply discourage people from *looking* for a possible

[1] *Christian Apologetics*, pp. 154 f. [2] *Ibid.*, p. 155. [3] *Ibid.*, p. 174. [4] *Ibid., loc cit.*

explanation: and indeed this might be the very effect desired by the predictor—guaranteeing that it should remain 'miracle' for an indefinite time. But how could anyone be so sure that certain events could not at some time be explained? The scientist does not claim that his present armoury of concepts and theories is adequate to account for every phenomenon. He is continually modifying, scrapping, replacing these in the interests of tidier hypotheses, theories of wider scope. He is committed only to a *method*, the formulating of hypotheses that are verified, and not falsified by experience.

It seems to follow that once we accept the definition of 'miracle' as 'awe-arousing anomaly', we cannot wriggle out of the possibility of eventual causal explanation of any once-miraculous event. If the event remains awe-inspiring after the explanation, it *could* still qualify as a miracle. But with practically all the New Testament examples, most of the awesomeness itself almost certainly results from the inability to explain. The one would tend to vanish with the other. Or, if not, the wonder that remained, say, at a healing miracle, would be of precisely the same order as our wonder at the twentieth-century surgeon's skill. But plainly the Christian wishes to see the works of Jesus as miraculous in quite a different sense, a sense we have not yet touched upon, but now must.

The point of Richardson's denial that science could explain all, is that he wants to find a way of seeing the miracles as in some special sense the action of God. This comes out very clearly in *A Theological Word Book of the Bible*.[1] There again we are reassured that miracles in theory are explainable according to laws as yet unknown. But then the miracle of the resurrection of Jesus is described as 'God's mighty act in raising him from the dead'. And this is simply to follow the Scriptures. Back in *Christian Apologetics*[2] Richardson considers certain rival, *incompatible* interpretations of the miraculous. Among these are (i) 'manifestations

[1] London: S.C.M., 1950. See articles on 'Miracle', 'Resurrection'.
[2] p. 173.

of the power and love of God', and (ii) 'the power of mind over nature', and (iii) 'unscrupulous trickery'. These could be incompatible, only if the first is taken as a *causal explanation* of miracles, like the other two theories. So in the resurrection account God is seen as somehow interfering in nature, in order to reveal his power in a way *different* from that in which any natural event reveals it.

Obviously the definitions from which we started have been left far behind. According to them, there is no reason why what we have called miracle may not turn out to have been trickery or explicable by psychical research. We should not have been wrong to call it 'miracle' while our ignorance lasted. But now we have seen the attempt to deny the *possibility* of explanation by the scientist, so as to guarantee that yesterday's miracle will not become tomorrow's commonplace. Further, Richardson has suggested that there are phenomena which lie altogether beyond the power of science to explain and require to be described as 'manifestations of the power and love of God'. To say this is to deny that the miracle is simply a wonder-generating anomaly, not as yet explained. It is to say that the miracle *has* an explanation—namely, the special intervention of God in the world. Only such a slide in meaning could account for the following sentence: 'Against all modern attempts to explain the resurrection as something natural and comprehensible . . . it is necessary to insist that the resurrection of Jesus is *miracle*, mysterious and irreducible, from the biblical point of view.' [1] On the old definition, this contrast *could not be made*—the contrast between the 'natural and comprehensible' and the miraculous. For according to that an event could be a miracle, and yet turn out to be natural and (in course of time) comprehensible. Nor could one say that any event was 'irreducibly' miraculous—except in the sense that it might be expected to evoke wonderment at all times, even though its explanation were found: otherwise, one could say only that its explanation was pending.

[1] *A Theological Word Book of the Bible*, p. 194.

The scientific 'perspective' forces Richardson to grant a theoretical natural explanation of miracles: the biblical perspective forces him to see God as himself causally initiating events in the world. The two perspectives war against each other. Can they be reconciled? We might try retaining both by saying: God is the author of certain events, rather as human beings are of other events. Then we could still say that miracles brought about by God would be law-abiding, natural, and theoretically explicable, as the original definition demanded. But that definition also demanded that once an anomaly was explained, it ceased to count as miracle. Once explain these events as God-initiated, and they would no longer be miraculous. Paradoxical; but entailed as soon as God is taken as causally intervening.

But at least it might be said, the intervention of God will remain awe-inspiring and thus allow us to go on seeing the events he initiates as miraculous (on the second count). I wonder if it would; once we had fully and rigorously thought through all it would mean to think of God in this way. For we should no longer be thinking of a God who 'infinitely transcends the world' (Tillich). We should be impairing that transcendence, were we to conceive God as causally operative upon nature in the same way as natural events are causally operative upon one another. Indeed, it is highly questionable whether we should still wish to call such a being God at all. Rather, we should have allowed (if we did so) a hard-won distinction between God and nature to lapse. Remember Professor Hodges' words quoted in the previous chapter. The conception of God is of a being

> incommensurable with all objects of our experience, and [this is an attribute] which it is hard to see as contributing to an explanatory hypothesis intended to account for particular facts.[1]

If, on the other hand, we are determined to take nothing away from God's transcendence, and refuse to think of him as causally

[1] Compare the 'religious objection' to the Cosmological Argument; Chapter Nine below, pp. 166 f.

intervening in the world, the difficulty now is to know how to infer from the 'awe-inspiring anomalous' to 'God manifesting his power and love'. There is certainly an immense gulf between the two. Many of the properties of liquid helium remain today surprising and anomalous: our definition entitles us to call them 'miraculous', and because of the history of the word 'miraculous', that would seem to entitle us also to say, 'God here specially reveals himself.' But this last inference is shut off from us, as long as we remain strictly within the terms of the definition, which says *nothing* about God, only about our present ignorance of explanations and our wonderment. It would be just as precarious to argue from the *latter*—the awe and wonder—to the claim, 'God is here revealed'; for how could one be in the least degree sure that a world made by no God might not contain sights and sounds which elicited these same responses?

'Coherence' can be appealed to here, however. The New Testament miracles are not unrelated, sporadic outcrops of odd happenings. They focus attention on a life and doctrine which have a pattern. Jesus is the second Adam, restoring what the fall of the first Adam had despoiled. Healings, feedings, the overcoming of death, are tokens of the divine redemptive work. We have therefore, on the Christian view, very much better ground for taking some central New Testament miracle as authentic than if it were one isolated, non-cohering tale about the remote past.

But what makes the pattern stand out? What is the background, so to speak; and what the contrasting colour in which the pattern is delineated? With the miracle-stories, doubtless, the striking thing is their running counter to our knowledge of nature. This (applying our definition) is due to our ignorance of the natural laws to which they actually conform. Allow a long enough time for research, and with the discovery of these laws the oddness would vanish. So would the pattern, in so far as the miracles contributed to it: just as the pattern of a rug would vanish, if it were all dyed one colour. This might puzzle the Christian, who sees his Gospel as for all time and all circumstances. But more worrying

still is the fact that on these assumptions, when we call miracles
'mighty works of God' we are referring to no more than the
divine sagacity in focusing our attention in certain events through
our ignorance of their (quite unremarkable) causes. There might
be nothing morally reprehensible in thus 'cashing in' on human
ignorance: but as an account of miracle it seems a very far cry from
what the Christian normally means by God's mighty works.

3

Not all biblical critics deny that it is possible to penetrate the
barrier between early Church and historical Jesus. Not all are so
pessimistic about recovering 'objective history' as are most of
those we have studied in these two chapters. Even if the Form
Critics are right in detecting common oral and literary shapes in
New Testament stories and 'words' of Jesus, it is still possible
that in part their *content* may quite authentically point back to
events which took place before the death of Jesus, and thus before the Church-tradition began its formal stereotyping.

The German scholar, Joachim Jeremias, for example, has tried,
in a study of the parables, to argue back from the New Testament
interpretation to the original spoken by Jesus. His method depends on his belief that the changes, embellishments, *etcetera*,
upon Jesus' own words took place in certain constant directions;
being expanded and modified so as to speak to the needs of the
Church in *its* own situation (not that of Jesus), and being
developed on allegorical lines, never favoured by Jesus himself.
'Allow off' for all these tendencies, and something like the original
parables can be reconstructed. The attempt, at any rate, is a fas-
cinating piece of detective work, although unlikely to revolution-
ize the whole historical problem. For one thing, it must *take for
granted*, and cannot itself establish, the general trustworthiness
of the New Testament picture of Jesus' life, with its successive
'situations'. Secondly, there is great room for speculative error in

deciding that if a parable seems to fit some situation in Jesus' life, then we have probably recovered its actual original setting. Nor can we check up independently on an assumption like, 'Jesus never used allegory.'[1]

Yet this sort of piece-by-piece attempt to recover objective history is by no means valueless, although its results are seldom spectacular. The fact that such research is not caught in an impasse, prevents one concluding that we have all the evidence we ever will have for or against historicity, and that therefore the Christian must build his faith upon the proclamation of the first-century Church and upon the 'existential' impact of proclaiming it today. Whether the theologian likes it or not, it keeps open the possibility of further confirming or falsifying what is proclaimed: it puts a question-mark against attempts to insure the Gospel against all objective-historical risks. Archaeological research plays exactly the same role.

It is, of course, quite another question, not our present concern, whether the objective history that *is* recovered is substantial enough to confirm critical events, like the resurrection.

4

Four general conclusions stand out at the end of these studies on historicity.

(i) In this field at least existentialist approaches are attractive but highly dangerous. The distinction between objective history and existential history is a valuable extension to our vocabulary, but it cannot bear the weight increasingly laid upon it by many theologians. In particular, its use leads to a sense of false security, an illusion that the risks of history can be and have been eliminated.

(ii) It is true that there must come a point at which detailed

[1] See Professor A. M. Hunter, reviewing *The Parables of Jesus*, in *The Journal of Theological Studies*, 1955.

historical analysis ends (temporarily) and a *verdict* is passed—to believe or not to believe. But the verdict, to be *just*, must be supported by the detailed historical conclusions; otherwise it is irrational. It may also require revision in the light of new evidence. Where the Christian Faith is on trial, appeals against former verdicts are always in place. Above all, the logical distinction between adducing evidence for the New Testament and pronouncing a verdict upon it, does not entitle us to any release from the 'anxiety of the historical'; any more than a jury's verdict relieves a court of appeal of the 'anxiety' of sifting over once more the evidence on which the original verdict was based, rightly or wrongly. The verdict cannot be floated off, detached from, the supporting evidence in such a way that it could remain unaffected, should the evidence alter or be reinterpreted after the verdict is passed. (To speak of being 'committed' to a faith is sometimes an attempt to do exactly this: once committed, one may feel no longer obliged to keep on the *qui vive* for new evidence pro or con. This again is comfortable, but intellectually dishonest.)

(iii) The intractability of the problem of *miracle* points to the deepest difficulty in *any* endeavour to point at God as the explanation of natural events. For this amounts to the problem of how a being who transcends the world can still be causally operative *within* the world. The problem is intractable, whether one says that miracles have 'natural causes' or that they do *not* have them. Different theologians, however, tackle these questions in so many different ways, that space has permitted us to discuss only the view of one influential writer—and that in the barest outline. On the basis of that discussion we cannot draw any general conclusions about the possibility of an intelligible theory of miracle.

(iv) As always, honesty demands keeping open the possibility that in view of the exiguous evidence in hand, scepticism is a more reasonable course than the erection of the dubious defences we have examined. The theologian says in all earnestness that there *must* be a way of escape from the anxiety of historical risk, for Christ is the bringer of peace. But we cannot lightheartedly dismiss that other and more austere thought—that because escape is *not* possible, Christ may not be after all so surely the bringer of peace.

CHAPTER EIGHT
SECULAR ETHICS AND MORAL SERIOUSNESS

I

'Do we need God as the ultimate explanation of moral experience?' We have recently seen a striking revival of interest in the relation of morals and religion, both from the practical educationalist point of view and from that of the theologian, who claims that here is one department of life in which the concept of God has undoubtedly a crucial explanatory role to play. But practice and theory cannot be kept apart in this topic. The theologian claims not only theoretical difficulties in accounting for morality without God, but he often holds that without religious belief moral seriousness is impossible; all the solemnity and authority of the moral law, even the moral dignity of humanity itself—all these go as soon as God is denied to be the author of that law. And without the expectation of eternal life morality is frustrated and mocked, loses all purchase over us. It is not simply that the sceptic finds himself bereft of the *prestige* that God brought to a way of life already and independently known to be morally good, nor that divine sponsorship made the good life (psychologically) easier to achieve. It is a matter of logic and 'theory of knowledge'—of what moral judgements *are*. Paul Ramsey states on the first page of his *Basic Christian Ethics* that 'God has something to do with the very *meaning* of obligation'.[1]

---

[1] Paul Ramsey, *Basic Christian Ethics* (London: S.C.M., 1953), p. 1; my italics.

What is being so frequently claimed, then, is that the man who fully realizes what morality is, why he should do his duty and what it is to do it, is already a theist—even if unknown to himself. Or again, it is to claim that if the sceptic completely saw the moral implications of his unbelief, he would prefer to doubt *any* speculative argument rather than live out, put into practice, those implications.

It should be noticed that, if this is a legitimate way of expressing the moral argument, certain questions of psychology are here not crucial. Quite a number of people *might* lose seriousness in carrying out morally right actions once they lost all belief in the prospect of final reward or punishment in a life hereafter. But before this could count as a moral argument, we should have to discover whether these people had ever clearly distinguished morals from 'prudentials'—whether their change of attitude did in fact result from change in the 'very meaning of obligation' or from the withdrawal of the prospect of 'pie in the sky' and of the fear of damnation. Our question is a *philosophical* one: can a secular ethic find the language in which the whole gamut of moral experience can be expressed without parasitic dependence on a dwindling Christian inspiration? or *must* it present a morally lop-sided picture of man which tempts him to destructive Satanic pride, denies him his dignity, terminates in his despair? If the latter is true, the theologian would have gone far to justify his claim that only on the hypothesis that God exists can moral experience in the largest sense be explained.

2

Few theologians now claim bluntly that moral principles are nothing but commands of God; or that the sole justification for obedience to any moral imperative is 'God commands it'. Most would agree, when pressed, that God ought to be obeyed because what he commands *is good*. On any other view we have the worship of power only, obedience to the strong, as strong. Nevertheless, sophisticated new versions of 'will-of-God ethics' abound in twentieth-century Protestant theology. Their apologetic aim is to intertwine moral and religious discourse so closely that no understanding of morality is possible without acceptance of its 'divine warrant'. Bonhoeffer argued in his *Ethics* that the notion of 'authority' is crucial to morals. If conflicting moral judgements are uttered, the one by a thoughtless child and the other by an adult with a great deal of experience of life, we are of course justified in paying more heed to the authoritative adult. The *summit* of authority is God, whose 'commandment is the only warrant for ethical discourse'.[1] Were there conflict between human and divine 'judgements' and should we have no moral insight into the rightness or wrongness of God's command, we ought analogously to submit to his supreme authority: for he alone possesses the full synoptic vision of human relations in all their complexity and can see the outworking, the immediate and remote consequences, of human action. 'In ethical discourse what matters is not only that the contents of the assertion should be correct, but also that there should be a concrete warrant, an authorization for this assertion. It is not only what is said that matters, but also the man who says it.' [2]

Grant an omniscient God, and much of this is incontestably true. The sceptic may readily agree that it is beyond *human* capacity to answer with finality questions about the long-term impact upon millions of people of, say, a radically new political policy or even of a startling increase in expectation of life. But does it follow from this that God's commandment 'is the only warrant for ethical discourse'? It is only by having direct moral insight into *some* at least of God's commands, by being able to judge these as morally worthy, that we could be justified in *occasionally* arguing that although we have no such insight in a particular case, we may be sure that God's will still ought to be done. Deny this, and we could no longer defend ourselves if

[1] Dietrich Bonhoeffer, *Ethics* (London: S.C.M., 1955), p. 244.
[2] *Ibid.*, p. 238.

130

someone protested in the following way. 'Incongruities between
our judgement and God's command,' he might say, 'may be due
not to our ignorance or creaturely limitations but to God's de-
ficiency of goodness.' Only after we had established God's goodness, by discovering that he consistently gave forth good commands, could we begin to invoke the argument from authority in
cases where we chose not to trust our own judgement. But if all
this is true, then it cannot be demanded that, before we accept any
moral principle, it should be shown to be commanded by God—
in order to give it 'authority'. For all that Bonhoeffer says, this is
one sense in which 'the commandment of God' *must* 'be replaced
by our own choice'.[1] There is therefore no apologetic force in
this argument from authority alone, for before we can know
whether or not we are in the presence of a morally *reliable* authority, we have to make and trust certain inescapable direct moral
judgements which cannot themselves be justified in terms of
authority.

3

It is sometimes claimed that we must go a good deal further than
this. Not only are we unable to come by reliable moral judgements without reference to divine authority, but moral judgement
of any kind is itself necessarily presumptuous, an exhibition of
sinful pride. Who is man to weigh up the commands of God in the
scales of his 'mere morality'? His sole fitting attitude is total
humility under the *divine* imperative, not under any self-imposed
moral imperative.

But it is relevant to ask the question: Ought we to obey God?
The Christian must consider this a proper question, to which he is
prepared to say unhesitatingly: Yes. If he is to continue *praising*
God for being good, he must believe that God *might* (without
logical contradiction) have been bad, *might* have issued commands

[1] *Ibid.*, p. 245. Bonhoeffer is not himself concerned here to use his argument apologetically: but it is often so used.

which ought not to be obeyed. (If not, there would be nothing to be thankful about.) The question is proper: but what does it mean? We can see that most easily by asking a fresh question, again a proper one: *Why* should God be obeyed? We cannot say: Because he is omnipotent, omniscient; for there is nothing logically improper in saying: He is omnipotent and omniscient *and* morally wicked. Obviously, the only sort of answer that would satisfy us is an account of certain *morally* relevant features of God's nature; for moral evaluations are shorthand ways of drawing attention to the presence of just such features, together with the expressing of attitudes favourable or unfavourable to them. Thus the moral evaluation of what we know about God's being and activity is once more inescapable—logically inescapable; for without it we cannot say 'God ought to be obeyed'. And if those words are denied us, there is no justification for humility under the divine imperative, other than considerations of prudence.

Despite their similar grammatical shape, 'moral imperative' and 'divine imperative' are not logically parallel phrases. They work in rather different ways. To say that the moral imperative ought to be obeyed is true but uninformative; for its truth follows from the meaning of the words 'moral imperative'. A moral imperative is the prescription of what ought to be done. The same cannot be said of the statement 'the divine imperative ought to be obeyed'. This is not true by definition, since divine commands *could* be wicked, if there were an evil deity. 'Divine imperative' is not logically different from 'managerial imperative', 'dictatorial imperative'. It ought to be obeyed only if what is commanded is right: the divine imperative is binding only if it coincides also with the moral imperative. To exhort people on moral grounds to renounce the moral in favour of the divine imperative is a logically absurd request.

Man, then, is not guilty of arrogance in retaining the right to defy God, should God command what is evil: if that right were renounced, he could no longer call the God of Christianity good. Further, if he is to call God good, it can only be by experience of his consistently good acts. One cannot go on *indefinitely* saying: This looks like cruelty, or callousness or indifference on God's part, but it *can't* be, since he is good; for we cannot know his goodness save through these and the like acts.

Nor can the appeal to underivative moral judgements be deflected into an acceptance *instead* of religious statements from which these seem to follow. Duty to love one's neighbour seems to follow from the doctrine that God is the common father of a single human family of brothers. But to state it like this, briefly, is to omit certain necessary steps in the inference. How *do* brothers behave to one another? Sometimes *un*lovingly. Are we then to imitate *all* facets of 'brotherly' relations? No; only those we *ought* to imitate—those which exemplify brotherly *love*. Thus before we can interpret the doctrine (see what is meant to 'follow' from it), we have to know *already* the moral conclusion towards which we are working.[1] The doctrine cannot relieve us of the need to judge morally by ourselves.

4

At this point an objector might say with great indignation, Are you implying that the New Testament teaching, contrary to the belief of two thousand years, is morally *irrelevant*, that we can accept its ethical instruction only if we previously and independently possess the insights it seeks to communicate? This is not in fact implied at all: any moral theory (religious or secular) must account for the occurrence of moral discovery and moral progress. The New Testament morality of love, of concern for purity of motive, the reversal of pharisaic 'virtues', may (and *should*) be taken as expressing a quite fundamental moral advance. The distinction, however, which needs to be emphasized is that between (1) taking these new judgements as moral advances and as also

[1] On this problem, see D. D. Raphael, *Moral Judgement* (London: Allen and Unwin, 1955), p. 80.

revealed by God (two logically independent points), and (2) acceptance of these as advances *because* revealed. It is only the second view that must be rejected; for moral insight cannot (we have seen) be reduced to insight into theological fact or divine command. But once this distinction is clearly made, the secular moralist may return to his New Testament, and without hypocrisy or 'double think' may study and try to implement in practice the way of life which it specifies. He will certainly not be able to accept every statement in it which the believer accepts; but the *moral* precepts and parables he *may* take as binding upon him, without inconsistency. Whether he succeeds in fulfilling them is quite another matter.

5

No amount of theological statements of fact can relieve men of the need to decide morally for themselves. What obligations we have, therefore, cannot be 'undermined' by God's non-existence. But the theologian may challenge that 'therefore': he insists that so enormous a change in one's conception of human life—its origin, its span—as is entailed by the transition from belief to unbelief, *must* have equally enormous repercussions upon moral beliefs also. In particular, to deny God is to deny that any man is ever assured of realizing the *summum bonum*: his own progress towards self-perfection is interrupted by death; likewise his efforts to achieve the well-being of others is subject to all the precariousness and fragility of existence unrelieved by any hope of life hereafter. The sceptic is quick to reply that this transition from belief to unbelief does not 'undermine' moral obligations, unless obligations are binding only if the good life is completely attainable. But in fact morality makes the same demands *whether or not* our ideals can be completely realized. Lying, stealing, or murdering is no whit more or less reprehensible if men are mortals or immortals, whether their way of life is to last a generation or all eternity.

not immediately satisfy the religious moralist.
says, *do* lost their bindingness, if unforeseen
context of their performance. A professional
igation to play (despite his contract), once his
the field: nor has an oboe-player, if three-
stra have walked off the platform. The setting
ions, as the religious man sees it, is that of
tion between man and God towards the van-
achievement of the supreme good. If you
is no God, he is like the footballer or the
rse plight—his vision of cosmic harmony is
his obligations are cancelled.

asibility in this line of thought: many con-
ts are dissolved in the persistent failure of
side of the bargain. But note that not all
ontracts or agreements demanding recipro-
eded by the signing of documents or the
ing. To come to the point, it would be an
hology to see *all* obligations as contracts
en more fanciful than seeing the state as
cal 'social contract'. Moreover, Christian
morality emphasizes the existence of a very important class of
non-reciprocal obligations—there must be no limit to forgiveness
of injuries, love not only for those who return it but for enemies
also. How then is the Christian, of all people, in a position to insist that all obligations are undermined if the good life cannot
completely be realized? Consider, finally, a statement like the
following: 'I ought to do what I can to relieve this child's misery
(or that old person's loneliness, or that animal's suffering),
whether or not there exists any God who can make amends hereafter for what is amiss here and now, and whether these beings
are mortal or immortal. All these speculations are (at the moment)
beside the point—misery (loneliness, pain) ought to be relieved:
that is enough.' One could make a case for saying that it is Christian insight as much as anything which has taught us to see such a

statement as morally noble. To revert to a demand for reciprocity, for complete realization of the good life, as a condition of having any obligations is to fall far below the New Testament's own most valuable teaching. And yet the Christian seems constantly tempted to do so.

6

Suppose the secular moralist is right in what he has so far claimed. It still does not follow that a non-religious ethic can legislate adequately for every aspect of life without covertly drawing upon Christian language and resources no longer his by right. Can he reckon in particular with what the Christian calls the fact of sin, with human capacity for love, with human dignity, and with 'the meaningfulness of life'? Christian moralists have cried on all counts, vehemently—No. It may be useful to discuss each of those points in turn, beginning with the problem of sin.

The charge against the humanist has often been that he is necessarily deprived of the dark colours of the palette. He chronically exaggerates man's ability to undertake social engineering without disaster: he is fondly utopian, for he no longer realizes that without God, and the Son of God, man 'can do nothing' [John 15. 5]. A sober and informed statement of this view can be found in Reinhold Niebuhr's *Christian Realism and Political Problems*.[1] Secular ethics and politics are bankrupt; their trust in perfectibility and progress has been shown up in our catastrophic century to be the sham it is. Human egocentricity has been fatally ignored. '. . . the belief that the power of man's lusts and ambitions is no more than some sub-rational impulse, which can be managed with more astute social engineering or more psychiatric help, lends an air of sentimentality to the political opinions of the liberal world'.[2] Among those vast arrogant social experiments of our time, Marxism most notably, 'proves that no one is good or

[1] London: Faber and Faber, 1954.
[2] *Op. cit.*, pp. 16 f. See also pp. 13 f.

wise enough to be completely entrusted with the destiny of his fellow-countrymen'.[1] Altruism in political reform 'degenerates into hatred for those who express their egotism in some ways different from our own'.[2] The only check is a return to the Christian consciousness of man's sinful revolt against God.

First, one must admit how strong a case Niebuhr has. Utopianism, revolutionary schemes of reform, have often indeed borne fruit far different from their originators' vision. Men *do* abuse the language of psychotherapy in evading responsibility for their moral blunders. They misuse equally the language of economics and politics in order to give an air of impersonality to their miscalculations. Cruelty and selfishness are called maladjustment: brutality and folly are labelled historical necessity. The question, however, is whether Christian dogma alone can express those judgements upon these evils and alone can offer effective counsel against them.

Niebuhr, within limits, himself suggests, No. As we quoted, our experience of Marxist communism *itself* 'proves that no one is good or wise enough' to play the utopian manipulator. This judgement has the form of a generalization from a 'crucial experiment' on a colossal scale. It can be empirically reached, without reliance on religious dogma. Revolutionary utopianism, it suggests, is self-stultifying as a policy: experience demands that it be modified to a *piece-meal*, *gradual* reform of state and society; that no single person or party or *élite* should be trusted with unlimited power. Granted the ability to reflect in this way upon experience, self-regulation in morals and politics is seen to be possible.[3] In other words, there is no reason why humanist morals should remain naïvely optimistic about humanity, in defiance of all such experience, and be unable to amend its policies in the light of them. The secularist may fail to *profit* from experience; but equally may the Christian fail to live out his creed in practice.

[1] *Op. cit.*, p. 20.   [2] *Ibid.*, p. 22.

[3] See Karl Popper's notable defence of the 'open society' in his book of that title (London: Routledge and Kegan Paul, 1945).

Second, the secular moralist is entitled to protest as vigorously as Niebuhr, when the technical jargons of sociologists and psychologists are used to deny that responsibility, blame, or punishment are ever in place—that all 'crime' proceeds from maladjustment or all wickedness from traumas of infancy. The error in each case is the extension of indispensable *specialist* attitudes to cover judgements of a general sort upon people—quite outside the specialist situation. Moral condemnation *is* out of place between a doctor and his patient. But that does not mean it never is *in* place. The sociologist is right to plan detachedly the improvement of environment as an aid to reducing crime. But again that does not mean detachment is *invariably*, and in every situation, the proper attitude. These illicit extensions can be and *are* deplored by sceptics as much as by Christians.[1]

If the first part of our question has been answered,[2] the second has not. Secular ethics may cope in theory with the potentialities of evil in men, but can it offer effective counsel against that evil, 'bring it home' to people as the vocabulary of sin and the Fall brings it home? This is a psychological or rhetorical question that can be assessed only in pragmatic terms. Which way of speaking makes the greater impact? At the present time traditional Christianity is in a quandary over this. On the one hand, it possesses unequalled resources of parable and precept, example, allegory, symbolism, as vehicles of its 'slant' upon human evil. On the other hand, the value of these resources is very much reduced because of the intellectual puzzlements that the same language generates, its entanglement in affirmations about a transcendent God, about his Son, Very Man and Very God, and about an outmoded, pre-scientific cosmology. The edge is taken off what is

[1] See, for example, Professor Antony Flew's interesting paper 'Crime or Disease' (*The British Journal of Sociology*, 1954).

[2] I know that the doctrine of sin has implications that go far beyond the need for caution and humility to which I have limited my discussion. This is at any rate a crucial part of the doctrine, and one that can be dealt with by itself without too much distortion.

being said about 'egocentricity' because of uncertainty over the status of the whole linguistic fabric of which it forms a part. Against this, the empiricist's claim gains in attractiveness, his claim to show why humility and caution are essentials, by pointing to the (very recent and dramatic) disasters that follow their neglect. This gain in directness and intelligibility at least compensates the loss of most of the resources of Christian language.

Some theologians, among them Brunner, would still deny that even this repudiation of utopianism, this retention of moral seriousness by the secular moralist, begins to do justice to all that the Christian believes (or ought to believe) about sin. No amount of *self*-regulation in politics or morals can remedy the impotence of a corrupted will. Humanity at the Fall suffered a dislocation of its moral life, turned from 'God-centredness' to 'self-centredness'. Far more than humility and caution are required to rehabilitate it in the way it should go. The most earnest moral striving is worthless: 'my duty to do good is precisely the sign that I cannot do it'.[1] The very sense of obligation, the tension between what we *should* do and what we *wish* to do, is evidence that goodness lies at 'an infinite impassible distance'.[2] Once more, surrender to God, obedience to His will, return to God-centredness are more realistic responses to the human situation than any reliance upon mere morality.

Three comments on this. First, if *strictly* we cannot make *any* reliable moral discriminations, if our judgement is radically corrupted, then (as we have already argued) no good moral reasons remain for obeying God's commands rather than those of anyone else. Moral judgement cannot be so very untrustworthy if we are to depend upon it (as we must) in making that boldest of all judgements—'God is morally perfect'.[3]

---

[1] Brunner, *God and Man*, p. 78.

[2] Brunner, *The Divine Imperative* (London: The Lutterworth Press, 1937), p. 74.

[3] We may recall at this point our discussion of H. H. Farmer's account of our recognition of absolute values: see above, pp. 39 ff.

Second, part of what is being said may be that as a matter of empirical fact people who *do* live Christian lives tend more than others to attain true goodness of character. There could be an apologetic point here: their attainment of goodness could be held as witness to the actuality of the God in whose direction their lives are orientated, and who alone could make possible their escape from self-centredness. Two flaws spoil this argument. First, the claim is empirically impossible to establish; for no criteria can satisfactorily discriminate between who is and who is not a Christian. Church membership obviously will not do, nor doctrinal adherence. To consider only those who show eminent altruism and self-forgetfulness in their lives and to ignore those whose religion is a sentimental source of comfort, a *retreat* from life, or whose Church work is an expression for a concealed, hard egoism—would go very little way towards verifying that strong claim. Moreover the sceptics (among them a good many Marxists) could amass a formidable list of martyrs to their cause, martyrs whose atheism denied them any compensatory hope of heaven.

The other difficulty can be brought out by asking how one could be sure of distinguishing the effects upon character of (*a*) belief in a God who in fact exists, and (*b*) belief (of equal earnestness) in a God who (unknown to the believer) does *not* actually exist. A pious mistake, the unfounded assurance that God did help the believer, that he constantly directed his paths, might psychologically produce exactly the same character-transformation as a *well*-founded assurance would produce.

A few pages ago I argued that the practical moral impact of the biblical teaching is for many people blunted by puzzlement over the meaning and truth of the dogmas in which it is set. Similarly—and perhaps even more seriously—the language we have seen used by Brunner, the emphasizing of human weakness and fallibility, the depreciating of the ethical, the yielding of primacy to the command of God, is itself not as trusty a weapon against arrogance as it is intended to be. For the less confidence a Christian has in moral reflection, the less he will wish to submit to a sober, humble investigation of a complex practical problem, to hear all the opinions of morally sensitive men, or to heed evidence as to the facts, which empirical 'secular' research may uncover. So he is tempted to terminate such scrutiny prematurely with an appeal to 'God's will' as it appears to him. The very solemnity of this appeal inhibits further minute, painstaking exploration of the situation—especially if such exploration is a task for a special science such as sociology, economics, or psychology; for these disciplines may in this religious context appear as threats to man's 'personal' status, reducing men to the status of statistical counters.

The Christian can legitimately retort that this path of degeneration has not been followed in a great many investigations by religious bodies in recent years into such problems as marriage and divorce, the morality of warfare, economic planning, and so on. In many of these, Christians and non-Christians have profitably interchanged ideas, have given due weight to conflicts of duties and delicate estimates of consequences. Agreed: but what *prevents* the degeneration can only be a series of reflections on the following lines. 'This policy is God's will . . . at any rate, so it seems to me. But if I am fallible in moral judgement, am I any *less* likely to be fallible in judging what is or is not the divine will? Let me therefore study most fully the situation under judgement and all the moral implications of that situation as they seem to me and to other morally sincere men. If I am finally persuaded that harm would come of the policy, I may decide, in the light of this, that it could not have emanated from God—for he would never command evil.' Nothing could be more reasonable: but the Christian who thinks in this way has plainly renounced his claim that the measure of sinfulness can be taken only by withholding from moral judgement any competence at all: and he can no longer invoke the doctrine of a radical corruption through the Fall as the *one* sheet-anchor against presumptuousness.

A note must be added on that contrast, beloved of the depreciators of 'mere morality', the contrast between 'man-centred' and 'God-centred' living. Whoever becomes a Christian, says

Brunner, is 'no longer . . . himself the centre of the picture, but God' is in the centre.[1] All secular moralities, this thought-model implies, are ultimately self-centred, despite all their pretensions to altruism. 'Every form of natural ethics is anthropocentric—man desires the *summum bonum* because it is "good" for him. . . . Even the ethic which takes duty very seriously is an ethic of self-righteousness. . . . The moralist who lives by duty also seeks himself, his moral satisfaction, his own moral dignity. . . . Natural ethics is dominated by the principle of self-seeking and self-reference. . . . In it, man . . . expects the good as the result of his own efforts. . . . This is the root of that which the Bible calls "sin". . . . It is precisely morality which *is* evil.' [2]

Countless apologetic publications and sermons testify to the popularity and influence of this metaphor of the 'alternative centres'. And yet, for plotting the relationships between religion and morality, a more distorting and logically confused image could scarcely be found. First, the notion of 'man-centredness' is radically ambiguous. Applied to *all* secular ethics, it presumably stands equally for a Kantian type of theory, in which action from a sense of duty takes primacy over all other springs of action—certainly over all self-regarding 'inclinations'; or for a 'utilitarian' type, which represents moral endeavour as aimed at maximizing human well-being—again by no means only in one's own person. But Brunner's image permits him to glissade from these to *egoism* without seeing how vital a distinction is thereby ignored. He moves (under the umbrella of the image) from 'every form of natural ethics is anthropocentric' to 'the moralist who lives by duty . . . seeks himself'—a statement which would horrify no one more than Kant! Morality may be 'man-centred' in that it has to do with *men*—with their joys, sufferings, loves, disappointments, but that gives one no warrant for holding that this man-centredness makes every moral agent an egoist *malgré lui*. Yet it is primarily by suggesting exactly this that Brunner succeeds in showing man-centred ethics to be the evil thing he believes. Second,

[1] *The Divine Imperative*, p. 78.   [2] *Ibid.*, pp. 68–71.

the image obscures the difference between (*a*) the *logically necessary* sense in which every moral judgement must be *somebody's* judgement, and therefore inescapably 'man-centred', even 'self-centred', and (*b*) the sense in which *some* judgements are self-regarding and some not—a question of their content, not their logical form. It is ludicrous to wax indignant about self-centredness in sense (*a*), for without it there can be no judgement at all: it is equally ludicrous on empirical grounds to claim that the judgements of all secular moralists are invariably self-regarding in sense (*b*). Brunner's case borrows its plausibility, its apparent self-evidence, from a slurring of the two senses, a failure clearly to distinguish them.

Suppose someone were convinced of God's existence and moral goodness. Then indeed he would be blameworthy if he ignored God's commands, made no efforts to trust and love this Being who so loved him. . . . In doing so he would not be abandoning the 'man-centredness' of his judgements (in sense (*a*)), although in another intelligible sense his life would be also 'God-centred'. For just as the phrases 'moral imperative' and 'divine imperative' are not opposites, because they are not logically parallel; so neither are 'man-centred' and 'God-centred' opposites or logical parallels. The orientation of a Christian whose relation with God is any other than blind servitude must be *both* man- *and* God-centred.

Third, the paradoxical conclusion, 'It is precisely morality which *is* evil', is reached by Brunner only by assuming that lines of moral deterioration which are *possible* within the context of a particular interpretation of ethics are not only possible but also are practically inevitable, and logically necessary. Conscientiousness is not only always *in danger* of toppling over into self-righteous legalism, but somehow *must* so degenerate. But this pattern is no more 'necessary' than that the Christian's humility should invariably become a subtly inverted pride through self-congratulation over his achieving it. It is quite another thing to say that (men being what they are) both patterns often occur.

Of course, those who employ the thought-model of the 'centres' do not hold consistently to these extraordinary implications that we have been unravelling. When not under its spell, they give morality its due, as often as not. Unfortunately, such qualifications as are made for the model are much less memorable than the model itself.

In this section I hope, among other things, to have shown, *not* that Christianity takes too gloomy, pessimistic a view of human moral capacity, but that nothing prevents the secular moralist from reckoning equally seriously with the dark side—even though he uses different language to express himself. The apologist who denies this, and who gives an appearance of logical conclusiveness to his denial, does so only by distorting the logic of moral discourse, by obliterating distinctions which in fact he himself needs to make in other situations and needs to make quite as urgently as his secular opponent.

7

The believer who claims that no secular ethic can account for the enormity of sin, may say precisely the same about the other end of the spectrum of human moral possibility—namely, deny that *love* is intelligible save upon certain theological assumptions. The first argument of this kind which we shall look at assumes once more that a non-religious ethic entraps a man in an impersonal legalism, that 'hinders him from seeing the other person as he really is, and prevents him from hearing the real claim which his neighbour makes on him'.[1] To the non-Christian, people are only 'cases': love is impossible. But the believer is released from this net: he is not concerned to 'educate, reform, provide for [his neighbour] on any abstract principle whatever': their relationship 'can never be formulated in any law': man acts towards man according to their unique needs. And now love is possible:

[1] Again, see *The Divine Imperative*, pp. 73, 79 f.

because the morality of 'I ought', of principle, has been superseded.

The appeal of this argument derives from the grotesque carica-
ture it gives of a moral agent. No one is obliged to interpose a
formulated copy-book maxim between himself and the person
with reference to whom he acts. No more is a chess-player compelled to find a written warrant in the rule-book for every move
he makes. His original or unconventional play may still proceed
according to principles. If challenged, the player could justify or
defend his move, by stating the (probably highly complex) principle on which he acted. But the possibility of defending himself
in this way against the charge of random or quixotic play removes
nothing from his direct, *non*-legalistic response to the various
phases of his game. In just the same way we may love certain
people, just as they are in themselves, and preface none of our
acts towards them by any citing of maxims. Yet if someone asked
us *why* we felt compelled to act as we did on some occasion, we
could perhaps list the features of the situation which determined
our choice and agree that any exactly similar situation would demand a similar response. That is, we invoke a 'universalizable'
moral rule (again a complex one, for a complex situation). This
does not make us 'legalists' in Brunner's sense. No over-simplified
maxim constrained us; nor was our 'neighbour's' personal distinctiveness in any way violated. To act 'within the moral law' is
no more than to be prepared to defend one's judgement by appeal
to features of the situation which make that judgement the appropriate one. The features can be as complex as human beings are
complex: so much the worse for the copybook maxim: but *not* so
much the worse for morality. In short, to adopt a moral standpoint
is perfectly compatible with relations of love.

The French Catholic philosopher, Gabriel Marcel, resorts
to a very different argument. To love someone, says Marcel,
is to say, 'Thou shalt not die.' Once consider the loved one as
mortal, as sometime to suffer complete annihilation, and love
cannot survive. Perhaps *pity* can, or tenderness or goodwill; but

these are not love. '. . . The spirit of fidelity . . . requires of us an explicit refusal, a definite negation, of death.' The 'silence' of the beloved one's death need not and must not be interpreted as non-being: to regard it so is a 'betrayal'. 'If death is the ultimate reality, value is annihilated in sheer scandal'; human communion would be destroyed at its very centre.[1] Marcel is aware that this is quite a different sort of argument for immortality from those based upon, say, mediumistic communication, historical evidence of Christ's resurrection, or even philosophical arguments like those of Plato or Aquinas. Nevertheless, he does speak as if this 'existential' analysis of love succeeds in making belief in immortality less unreasonable. For all his qualifications, he means it to have apologetic value.

I am tempted, however, to see in it only an extended euphemism. A scale could be constructed between (*a*) 'realistic' but brutal description of death: 'X whom you loved is dead. To be dead is "to lie in cold obstruction and to rot" . . .', and (*b*) a gentle refusal to think of death as more than absence. Love is not ended but temporarily interrupted; there is still a felt continuity of relationship through 'fidelity' to the loved one. But it does not follow from our ability to see death in a variety of such ways that the way most favourable to the maintenance of love should be the only *valid* way, or indeed anything more than nostalgic wistful thinking. The spirit of fidelity *may* demand of me 'a definite negation of death'. But, alas, death may not choose to be negated. 'I can call spirits from the vasty deep.' 'Why, so can I or any man; but will they come when you do call for them?' The argument cannot establish Marcel's conclusions. But need we even assume his premises—that recognition of mortality is incompatible with love's survival? Human relations apart, people *do* value transient things; a sunset, a fleeting optical effect on a landscape, the execution of a ballet movement that lasts a few seconds. Perhaps for some people love of the transient never escapes a certain

[1] *The Mystery of Being* (London: The Harvill Press, 1951), Vol. II, p. 153; *Homo Viator* (Aubier: Editions Montaigne, 1944), pp. 205 ff., 211.

sadness: but the sadness does not defeat the love, save sometimes when one takes final leave of a landscape known over years or watches a ballerina, who will not, for some reason, be seen again. But all human encounters are not, mercifully, death-bed partings. Only if they were so, and if we ourselves alone did not *share* the mortality that takes others from us, would love for most people become too hard, too poignant, to bear. And this would still be no more than a *psychological* impediment to love, not the quasi-philosophical impediment Marcel seems to discover.

Awareness of mortality may even intensify love, not destroy it. And the intensification need not take the form of a *carpe diem* sensuality, a throwing off of moral restraint. For if such indulgence brutalizes and obliterates personal distinctiveness, blunts the very senses indulged, then there is just as strong ground for shunning it on assumptions of mortality as on assumptions of life everlasting.

8

What would it be like, the Christian sometimes asks himself, to lose belief in man's divine origin, in his 'calling' to sonship with God, in his immortality? It seems to him very often that to lose these would involve loss also of all human dignity and the draining of all meaning from life. T. S. Eliot has put it bluntly: 'If you remove from the word "human" all that belief in the supernatural has given to man, you can view him finally as no more than an extremely clever, adaptable and mischievous little animal.' Deny God and hereafter, and the difference between man and the animals seems no longer important. If this is true, is every sincere upholder of man's dignity and uniqueness a theist in fact, whether he label himself Christian or agnostic? On this view the apologist's task would be to show the sceptic that his scepticism, thank God, does not go deep; and to recall him from an unconfessed to an overt faith. This is the third charge to be considered against the competence of a non-religious ethic.

Is it being said, to start with, that it would no longer be important to *treat* people differently from animals? that their moral, aesthetic, and intellectual capacities might fittingly be ignored, as if non-existent? But it is a mystery why in an excess of self-punishment, we should add to the loss of religious belief the further loss of decency, goodness, concern for beauty, and truth. Men would continue to carry (along with their mortality) sensitivity to pain, responsiveness to love, delight in the arts, curiosity about nature. Nothing would have been proved against the reasonableness of *accentuating* the differences between man and the animals—even *although* both are mortal, and have their origin in a common 'life-process'. Differences remain in plenty. Undoubtedly one *can* view man as an 'extremely clever, adaptable and mischievous little animal', and (with the imaginative assistance of poets, novelists, dramatists, painters) as countless other things also. But to admit that imagination is versatile is a far cry from agreeing with Eliot that to the sceptic only *one* picture remains authentic. If man is not an immortal spirit, he does not have to be an animal. That he may be a *man* is less of a platitude than it might seem.[1]

People like Eliot, however, do not simply mean that the sceptic ought to ignore the differences between men and beasts. They feel that, independent of all human choosing, heeding, and ignoring, the denial of Christian doctrine alters, in some objective sense, the *value* of humanity. Humanity, in the universe as Christians interpret it, possesses as a matter of fact a worth, a nobility, which stands or falls with that interpretation alone.

The moralist has to protest here that this kind of language very easily warps and distorts our understanding of the concept of 'value'. It suggests that values are price-tags, affixed authoritatively on the objects evaluated. The Great Evaluator may, at his

[1] Compare Gilbert Ryle, *The Concept of Mind* (London: Hutchinson's University Library, 1949), p. 328.

pleasure, remove such price-tags, or down-value them as at sale-time, and so on. The value of human beings, that is, can be *read off* the appropriate price-tag. If we were mistaken in the belief that God settled human value in this way (that is, if God does not exist and thus did not 'set all things under men's feet'), then we were equally mistaken in believing that men possessed value, dignity, or nobility. The price-tags had never been affixed after all. What grounds could we have any longer for claiming that he *does* possess value?

The same gloomy implications do not follow, if we speak not of value and dignity as queer sorts of *things*, but of 'valuing', 'esteeming', 'holding in regard', as activities which men can always undertake if they so choose. To confer value is simply to hold dearly. To emphasize this aspect of valuing is a hint that it may not be paradoxical to go on esteeming humanity in the absence of divine price-tagging. Valuing is a process logically independent of describing: the sceptic will *describe* his world differently from the Christian, but that does not entail that he should *evaluate* the human world differently. Had there been a divine blue print of the good life for men, men themselves would have had to endorse *it*, hold *it* in esteem (or reject it, should it have been a bad one), before making its evaluations their own in a moral fashion. If there is no blue print and no God, they are not precluded from endorsing a scheme of values which still accords dignity to mankind in general and to certain kinds of human activity in particular. To ask, 'Does man lose his dignity if Christianity is not true?' suggests strongly that God, heaven and hell, and human dignity are all in the same sense items in the furniture of the universe, as the Christian sees it; and that the sceptic, the rascal, is denying that any of them exists.

'Does man lose his dignity . . .?' Ask, rather 'Is there any being to which I might reasonably accord *greater* value than man?' and, concerning particular judgements, 'Why should I esteem this act of heroism, self-sacrifice, devotion any the less, although there exists no God, or deny dignity to beings capable of the things men

149

are capable of?' No logical blunders are being committed if I say that dignity can be accorded to men on account of their freedom to pattern their own unrepeatable lives, on account of their courage in face of their finitude, the reality of death, and their capacity for living the moral life and the aesthetically creative life.

Or has something quite essential been left out of account? Grant that valuing is *according* value, deciding to hold precious, still, a critic may say, it matters tremendously *who* does the valuing. Here is the humanist's characteristic blasphemy—dignity is ours, he is claiming, if we choose to confer it upon ourselves, whereas, what dignity properly belongs to us can be accorded by God alone, as the conferring of a supreme honour.

Examine, then, this language of conferring honours. In normal contexts, when we speak of someone receiving, say, an academic honour, we are entitled to ask what were the *grounds* of his award. If these are unsatisfactory or undiscoverable, we challenge the worthwhileness of the honour conferred. Similarly, Christians usually admit that God's choice of man for special dignity in the hierarchy of being is not unrelated to the sort of creature man is: the presence of his distinguishing characteristics makes his award appropriate in a way it would *not* be appropriate if man were altogether a different kind of being.

Suppose, now, there is no actual conferring of dignity by God, since God does not exist. Those characteristics of man which *might* have been the grounds for a possible divine conferring are unchanged, and can serve the secular moralist as grounds for his own judgement.

This conclusion may still be contested. Man does *not* deserve the honour and dignity in which God invests him, some will say. Herein lies God's love for man as sinner. The humanist, however, does not have to claim foolishly that men consistently (or even *often*) live up to their capacities for noble conduct. He has not denied that their behaviour at times belies their dignity. To claim dignity on man's behalf is to speak of human *potentialities*, of an ideal only rarely approximated, not to describe his average actual behaviour. If the honour is not merited by man because of his revolt against God, that does not imply that humanity is quite without the features that could serve as a ground for the conferring of dignity: it means no more than that the realization of his potentialities has been thwarted. Even if his rebellion were to make it inappropriate to confer dignity upon him, it would not make it inappropriate in the same sense of the word as it would be to confer dignity upon a beetle or a sardine.

If dignity can be reclaimed, is the same true of 'the meaning of life'? I think it is: but an adequate attempt to answer this question, to clarify the logic of 'meaning' in this connection, would require a detailed separate study.[1] All I shall attempt here is to show that arguments of the form 'Reject Christianity and the meaning vanishes from life' rest on a misreading of that logic, or at least upon an artificial restriction on the use of the phrase 'the meaning of life'.

This restriction consists in assuming that life can have one and only one meaning: that what it 'means' to you it will also 'mean' to me, if I am fortunate enough to discover that meaning. For life to have meaning, goodness must finally be vindicated and triumphant; human ideals, strivings, aims must admit of ultimate realization. No personal disaster, deprivation, must remain sheer unredeemed loss. Deny that such fulfilments can be relied upon, and up goes the cry, 'The meaning is being emptied out of life.'

Yet it is odd to assume that, while words can be ambiguous, even have *many* strands of ambiguity, the meaning of *life* must be quite unambiguous. In everyday contexts we do speak of a *variety* of ways in which life can 'mean': people find 'new meaning' in life (in a new project, changed personal relations, or through coming to see a pattern that gives unity to their lives: see autobiographies like those of G. K. Chesterton, Arthur Koestler, or

[1] For some tentative discussion of this, see again *Aristotelian Supplementary Volume*, 1956, pp. 14 ff. Also Chapter Eleven below.

W. B. Yeats). 'Meaning' suffers temporary losses, temporary recoveries, in ways very closely related to the loss or retention of *initiative*, purposefulness, or 'command', a rejection of passivity, an ability to cope with whatever occurs. There is an important sense in which the hero of a great tragedy, an Othello, a Hamlet, even when confronted by the prospect of his immediate death, and having no hopes of a hereafter, may so retain initiative as to make nonsense of any suggestion that for him in his crisis life has lost its meaning.

In other words, the phrase 'the meaning of life' is not logically parallel to, say, 'the meaning of "kitten" '. Life may possess not one but countless meanings. And since it is not the meaning of a *word* that is being asked for, we have no reason to assume that life 'means' in the same way as a word (even an ambiguous word) 'means'. Neither resort to dictionaries nor appeal to ordinary discourse is an appropriate way of discovering what meaning life can have for a person in a particular situation. Rather, the agent must ask himself: How can I make order of this chaos, exchange passivity for a regained initiative, harness all my resources to meet whatever challenge I am encountering? If we are to speak strictly, meaning is *given* to life by individuals, not *discovered*. There is no single setting of life that grants meaningfulness, while all others take it away. In this the logic of 'possessing meaning' closely resembles that of possessing value or dignity. We may change our beliefs about the world most radically, without necessarily losing *either* 'possession'.

What is it that makes the Christian still so reluctant to admit that life may be meaningful to the sceptic, that meaning can be found within a finite and bounded life? It may be that he sees so wide a gulf between what that meaning could be for the sceptic and what it is to him. For his vision is of a universe in which human purposes and God's purposes for the whole cosmos are significantly related. The universe, outside man's own little world, is not bleakly indifferent to the drama of his existence. The back-cloth it offers is the well-devised work of a craftsman

Drowned head... "To sea of Earth
Was me, but at the full around earth's shore
So like the pulse of a input pulse hurled.
But was I only hear
In melancholy, long, withdrawing roar,
Retreating, to the breath
of the night wind, down the vast edges drear
And naked shingles of the world.

Ah, love, let us be true
To one another! for the world, which seems
To lie before us like a land of dreams,
So various, so beautiful, so new,
Hath really neither joy, nor love, nor light,
Nor certitude, nor peace, nor help for pain;
And we are here as on a darkling plain
Swept with confused alarms of struggle & flight,
Where ignorant armies clash by night."

(Turn to other people
at the garden)

who intends man to occupy the centre of the stage. The point can be brought out by likening the Christian's world to a room whose every piece of furniture, every utensil, every object within reach, is designed to minister to human wants. In contrast, the sceptic's universe is more like a cave strewn with random-shaped stones, where if anything lends itself to human needs it is only fortuitously so. Both analogies are caricatures, but the contrast is plain.

If the Christian insists on setting aside the word 'meaningful' for his own 'teleological' vision, no one can prevent him. Nor could one prevent a person from setting aside the word 'evangelist' only for preachers who converted at least one hundred souls per sermon, or the word 'chauffeur' only for uniformed drivers of Rolls Royce cars. Let no one imagine, however, that if he insists on using any of these terms according to these re-definitions, that he will mean the same thing as his hearers when he says, 'That preacher is not a real evangelist, even though he gained thirty converts last week', or, 'I know he drives the Director's Humber: that doesn't make him a chauffeur,' or finally, 'To the sceptic, life just *cannot* have any meaning.' In each case the hearers will be misled; for they, reasonably enough, assume that these words are being used in their ordinary, not in these artificially restricted, senses.

I am postponing to the last chapter a fuller discussion of what life can mean to the sceptic; in particular, what it can mean to the reluctant sceptic who has a 'naturally religious mind'. The present argument has attempted simply to show that the ambiguity and logical complexity of the expression 'the meaning of life' rule out those most common apologetic tactics—the claim that meaningfulness stands or falls with theological belief. *Certainly* the Christian who loses his belief, and with it his imaginative vision of the world, has a colossal reorientation to carry out. He may feel like a child who has awakened not in the familiar, friendly nursery in which he fell asleep, his parents within easy call, but in a desolate wilderness where no one knows of him, no one answers his cry.

The logical possibility of imparting fresh meaning to life is one thing: its practical difficulty quite another. When this task comes to be faced, the click-clack of logical analysis ceases to be helpful. Our need then is not a calculating machine, but those very different things—imagination and practical wisdom.

CHAPTER NINE
GOD AND COSMOS (I)

———

I

HISTORY and moral experience are by no means the only features of our world that have been held to demand God as their ultimate explanation. Many apologists have trained their spotlights not upon those, but upon the design and order of nature or upon natural beauty as even more urgently requiring belief in a divine Author. One most famous argument stands somewhat apart from all these attempts to infer God's existence from this or that *restricted* set of phenomena, namely the 'Cosmological Argument'. It takes as its starting-point the *whole* of phenomena, the world, the universe, the cosmos, call it what you will. Because there is a world of *limited* things, it must owe its existence to an *unlimited* being. Because everything we see or touch is *conditioned* by things outside itself, there must exist one totally *unconditioned* being. Because everything we know needs to be explained in terms of activity other than its own, *something* must exist whose being is its *own* explanation.

This is the path of argument followed by St Thomas Aquinas in the first three of his famous 'Five Ways' or demonstrations of God's existence. This is also the argument refurbished today by the Roman Catholic and Anglo-Catholic 'neo-scholastics', a most powerful group among theologians. If it is an abstract and dry argument, it more than compensates for that by its apparently quite invulnerable premiss, which states simply that there *is* a world—a world of limited things. It is not, therefore, exposed to falsification in the same obvious ways as were the arguments to God from particular historical events, and the argument from moral experience. In *those* cases the arguments fail, if the historical evidence is shown to be inadequate, or if morality is reinterpreted in a manner that no longer demands divine underpinning. In addition, unlike those arguments, the Cosmological Argument is brief, and (at first glance at least) logically transparent.

Philosophers of language, however, have tended to look with great suspicion upon an argument so boldly metaphysical as this. The argument is metaphysical in that strongest (and most abhorred) sense: it tries to infer an unobserved and unobservable entity from some highly general fact about the world. But, on the other hand, theologians who use it are at least prepared to *argue*. They remain in the same sphere of discourse as the philosopher: communication with them is very much easier than with the theologians of 'existential leaps' and 'ineffable encounters'. Yet, although new interpretations of the Argument are constantly being produced today, philosophers, for their part, are failing to grapple with these in discussion as seriously as they ought. Why should this be so?

The main reason is that a great many philosophers are convinced that the Cosmological Argument was once and for all demolished by Kant and Hume, and that restatements of it are no more significant of life than the twitchings of a body already dead. I believe, moreoever, that these philosophers are more nearly right than they are wrong. The Cosmological Argument did receive at least crippling wounds from Kant and Hume. And yet, because the Argument has not really a single form, but is more accurately described as a *cluster* of arguments, Protean in variety, philosophers have still the task of examining the claim that *some* versions are immune to these critical thrusts.

It is almost equally important to reckon with the battery of supporting reflections—what I shall call 'auxiliary arguments'—that are deployed by apologists, in order to give imaginative and intellectual stiffening to the bare skeleton of the Cosmological

Argument itself. These auxiliaries are often decisively important in determining whether the main line of reasoning will be found acceptable or not. This is particularly true, where the Cosmological Argument is taken not primarily as a rigorous formal proof, but as an aid to adopting a certain cast of mind, to feeling a sense of the precariousness of everything finite and contingent, and thus of their 'need' for divine undergirding.

Our study will divide up in this way. First must come a statement of certain versions of the argument: then an outline of the main line of refutation by philosophers of language. I shall follow that with some more sophisticated re-formulations of the Argument, aimed at evading the stock criticisms. These will be assessed in turn: and finally we shall look at one or two of the 'auxiliary' arguments, to see how well or badly they function.

2

Things, say the Thomists, are moved by other things and also cause movement themselves. They have both passive and active aspects. But a thing moves only if something else has moved it; and things are able to be active only if conditions in their environment permit them to be active. There is no logical end to the repeating of the questions, 'What made *this* thing move, or change, or develop?' or, 'What made it possible for *that* to be active?' The first question initiates a regress of 'thing moved by thing moved by . . .', and the other question starts off a regress of conditions under which movement (in this very wide sense of the word) is possible at all. According to the Thomist, both questions lead in the end to God. It is impossible that *everything* should be engaged in passing on movement received from something *else*. An unmoved mover, namely God, must be accepted to make sense of the fact of change. Second, it is impossible that everything should be dependent on something else for its capacity to act (as I am dependent on pen, desk, chair, heat from the sun . . .

in writing at this moment). If *everything* were like me in this respect, how could it be that any movement or change could be taking place, as it undoubtedly is, at the present moment? Again, we require to posit God as the one being on whom all depends, but who himself depends on nothing outside himself.

High up in the circus-tent a light picks out a clown, standing on a ball, balanced by a sea-lion, perched on a box. . . . The ground is in darkness, but we know that someone or something *must* nevertheless have its feet on the ground.

If you suggest to the Thomist that the regress of causes and conditions may be *infinite*, for all we know—and that therefore it may *not* demand an unmoved mover or first cause, he will reply that this sort of regress would be for ever unable to explain how there in fact *is* motion here and now, and how there *are* conditions that make activity possible here and now.

This stress on 'what is evident to the senses here and now' is important: for, despite the speculative daring of the argument, it is held to have its roots *in experience*. St Thomas said, 'It is *evident to our senses* and certain that in the world some things are in motion . . .' and '*Among phenomena we discover* an order of efficient causes. . . .'[1] Thomists are confident that their arguments make ample concessions to empiricism, while going on to draw out explicitly what experience knows only in a confused way. This, they believe, is a vital and largely neglected part of the metaphysician's task today.

I have just quoted the opening sentences of St Thomas's First and Second Ways. It is from these Ways that we have so far taken our statements of the Argument. The Third Way is currently even more highly thought of; and it too begins with an empirical premiss. 'We observe in our environment how things are born and die away'.[2] What does St Thomas think follows from that? Things that come into being and go out of being again can be said to 'happen' to exist. With any one of them you choose, it always makes sense to say, 'It *might* not have existed at all.' As a

[1] *Summa Theologica*, 1a. ii. 3.   [2] *Ibid., loc. cit.*

recent translator of Aquinas so well puts it, these things are all 'might-not-have-beens'. The core of the argument is this. *Not* everything, says St Thomas, could have been a might-not-have-been. Otherwise at some time nothing whatever would have existed. But if this has been so, nothing would exist today. (An utter, universal 'gap' in existence would be irrevocable.) We are compelled, then, to say that *something* must exist 'necessarily' (not just *happen* to exist). And that being is God. God is no mere contingent item of nature: for every item in nature hovers between being and non-being. But the non-being of God is unthinkable.

Many variations on this Third Way can be found in recent apologetics. Finite being, we are told, requires infinite being as its Ground. The drama of mutability is played out against a backcloth of immutable being, being that cannot *not* exist. Combining all three ways, we may say that the world as we know it is fragmentary and dependent, a vast pointer to a being who is self-explanatory, dependent on nothing, giving being to all, but himself receiving it from no source but himself.

Rather than present the Arguments formally we may prefer to look on them as levers by which to prise ourselves out of our habitual reluctance to see any mystery in the world's existence. Stop looking at things simply from a utilitarian standpoint. Stand back and stare. And it will dawn on you that the sheer fact of its existence is a great wonder. We may see it too as a 'suppliant for its existence' [1] on a being that has a different mode of existence from itself. If we do see it in this way, the arguments will have done their work.

[1] M. C. D'Arcy, *The Nature of Belief* (London: Sheed and Ward, 1931), pp. 258–262.

3

The current critics of the Cosmological Argument detect logical trouble in several places. One important ground of offence is the use it makes of the words 'cause' or 'move' (in the transitive sense). The vocabulary of 'cause' and 'effect', they argue, is useful to us in various familiar ways. We use it to remind ourselves and others of reliable procedures for manipulating our environment. We use it for summing up regular patterns of events, which we find by experience always to occur together, or to *vary* together in a predictable manner. The critics reject crudely mechanistic ideas of causality, which regard a cause as a quasi-material 'coupling' between adjacent events; one event pulling the next behind it like linked railway wagons. They equally avoid any view that reduces the relation of cause and effect to one of strict logical entailment, the effect being in principle deducible *a priori* from knowledge of the cause. The procession of events is neither like the march of a chained slave-gang, not like the rational unfolding of an argument.

If these philosophers are right, and if what we might call the natural habitat of 'cause' words is the ordering and grouping of our experiences and the manipulating of what is to come, then we can understand their distrust of the use made of those words in the Cosmological Argument. For if we argue from the existence of a world to a First Cause, we are not in this case recording some observed concomitance of events, or stating a causal law according to which certain sets of events vary reciprocally. We are instead *uprooting* the vocabulary of cause and effect from its habitat in the language, in order to relate the known *to the unknown and unknowable*. It is not the case that every time we have observed a universe, we have noticed a First Cause causing it, and that therefore we feel justified in saying, 'No universes without First Causes.' The transplanting of ideas here is all the more worrying when we begin to cast doubt (as we shall) on the meaningfulness of talking about 'the world' as the sort of thing that *can* have a cause. Whereas cause-words have their use in our language in the relating of limited thing to limited thing, the Cosmological Argument puts them to the work of relating an *infinite being* to the *totality of things*. It is from just such redirections of linguistic labour that breakdowns in meaning constantly occur.

'Why all this anxiety?' the defender of the Argument may reply. 'All that we have to know is that *every event has a cause*. We do know that: and it makes no difference *what* events we are talking about nor how hard it is to conceive the cause which they require. And so the world requires God as its cause. The argument is perfectly sound.'

'Every event has a cause.' What kind of a statement is that? To bear the load which the Thomist is now laying on it, it must be taken not merely as 'on the whole' true, or 'likely to be' true, but true without exception, *certainly* true. But if we are to argue from it to the existence of God, it must be also an *informative* statement, not a tautological or trivial one, like 'If it's raining, then it's raining.' I think it can be shown, however, that if we interpret this statement so as to make it certain, we are forced, by the same procedure, to make it *trivial*.[1]

What makes one so confident that this is an *informative* statement is that it looks at first sight so vulnerable to falsification. Could we find even one single event that had *no* cause, that would suffice to discredit it. And it would surely be an impressive bit of news about the world, if no such causeless event *could* be produced. So it looks as if our confidence in the truth of 'Every event has a cause' could be reasonably interpreted as implying that no causeless events have in fact turned up, so far as we know.

Yet this is unconvincing, for the following reason. Suppose that we had searched exhaustively for the causes of a certain event, and failed to find any. Would this entitle us to say at last, 'Here

---

[1] I am borrowing here extensively from the argument of G. J. Warnock's ' "Every Event has a Cause" ', in *Logic and Language* II, edited by Antony Flew (London: Blackwell, 1953).

is an instance that clearly refutes the statement, "Every event has a cause"?' No: anyone who wished to go on believing the statement to be true could and would say, 'We have just not *located* the cause here yet, but there quite certainly *is* one. Blame our experimental techniques or our lack of patience; but don't regard the statement as falsified.' But if this is to be our response in all situations of this kind; if we are always to brush off their challenge by saying, 'cause not yet found', instead of, 'maybe no cause here to find', then it is not nearly so clear that, when we say, 'Every event has a cause', we are saying anything momentous and informative about the world we live in. To go on saying it begins to look a little more like stubbornness on our part and less like commendable tenacity. Putting it another way: our statement begins to be used vacuously, from the moment we begin to deny that anything will count against it.

But it does not *sound* vacuous or empty. How account for its appearance at least of momentousness? This can be explained by the fact that the statement borrows meaning from certain *most* informative and really momentous (but different) statements. Among these is the statement that to an astonishing extent regular patterns of concomitant events can be detected in nature, that highly general laws can be formulated which describe these patterns and enable the prediction of future phenomena. But reports of the scientists' discovery of nature's orderliness, and the statement, 'Every event has a cause', are not identical by any means: nor does the first imply the second. Individual uncaused events might occur from time to time without in any way upsetting our overall picture of orderliness, and yet they would suffice to falsify the philosopher's statement that every event has a cause.

The Thomist will refuse to let this be the last word. He will now bring out his trump card and claim that the critic has quite misrepresented his crucial statement about causality. Of course no empirical fact could count against it: but this is only because it is not an empirical assertion in the first place, but a metaphysical one, and one which so taken is exceptionally fruitful. I suspect, however, that to re-label the statement in this way gives the defender only a verbal and temporary advantage.

In the first place: we are looking to the Cosmological Argument to furnish a certain kind of satisfaction by explaining the world through its causal dependence on God. The Argument leads us to expect that *this* satisfaction is homogeneous with the satisfaction provided by causal explanations generally, in everyday life and in science. St Thomas's empirical premisses ('It is evident to our senses . . . that . . . things are in motion', etc.) give us licence to believe that the sort of demand the cosmos makes for an Author is the *same* sort of demand as finite events make upon finite events for causes and conditions. And thus we cannot strengthen (or even save) the Cosmological Argument by driving a deep wedge between empirical and metaphysical causalities.

In the second place, when the scholastic says that 'Every event has a cause' is not a vacuous statement, but a fruitful, pregnant metaphysical one, we do well to watch closely lest he indulge at this point in circular reasoning. He may not be compelled to do so; but there are strong pressures in this direction. What, we must ask him, *makes* the statement momentous and fecund? By far the most tempting answer is this. 'It is fecund, because if we believe that every event has a cause we seem forced to pose the question of a First Cause for the world: it is momentous, because it makes belief in God inescapable.' But if we make its fecundity our ground for retaining it, if that is primarily what we *mean* by its fecundity, then we are certainly reasoning in a circle. For in that case, any proposition would qualify as fecund, if it entailed God's existence, whether the proposition were plausible or implausible. No matter what it asserted, it would have to be accepted as true, and momentously true!

That is to say, the theologian cannot rely on *that* sort of 'fecundity' to justify his use of 'Every event has a cause' as a metaphysical statement. He may, however, deny that this religious fecundity *is* his reason for holding the statement: he may deny in fact that any justification is required for it at all. He may fall back on saying that he 'just knows' that every event has a cause, and on 'just knowing' that this is not a vacuous utterance. If he digs his heels in here quite stubbornly, we cannot argue to any profit with him; although it may look initially as if we could.

Initially; yes. But it is not hard to show that the way is soon blocked. Consider, for instance, certain classes of happening that some people have claimed are uncaused, happenings that seem to count against the truth of 'Every event has a cause', if the statement is used non-vacuously. The freedom of the will is believed by some people to involve 'uncaused events' by moral agents; the phenomena of quantum mechanics constitute another sphere where the question, 'What caused this or that particular event?' is not always in place. If we accept the hypothesis of 'continuous creation', it may not be possible to ask what causes the creation of each new atom. They may just 'pop into being'. Could we not argue with the scholastic on the ground that in a universe where these or *some* of these causeless phenomena may have to be admitted, it will not do any more to say that every being simply transmits the causal impetus passed on from some other being? In fact, it would no longer be true in the completest sense that (in St Thomas's words) 'we *find* an order of efficient causes'. If we are really holding the statement 'Every event has a cause' non-vacuously, this should matter very much. For it implies that the Cosmological Argument loses all its rigour. There is now admittedly a class of non-caused events: and we may be hard put to it to show that 'the cosmos' itself is not a member of that class.

But the scholastic's way of meeting the challenge of that possible class of events reveals how little he really is perturbed by the thought of it. Take, for example, the 'indeterminacy principle' of the physicists. The physicist finds himself able to predict with considerable accuracy how many clicks a Geiger counter will make in a given time, as it records the activity of sub-atomic particles. He is *un*able to state when any *individual* click will take place, or to assign a cause to it when it has taken place. Discussing this, Dr E. L. Mascall admits that the positivist will say of the particular click—'It just happens.' But the theist, he says, denies that *anything* just happens. God's direct, 'primary' causality determines the moment of the click, although it has no *natural* cause.[1]

Now, what right has the theist to deny that some events just happen, uncaused? It looks as if Dr Mascall is eliciting that right from his belief that every occurrence must be ultimately caused by God's activity. But if so, we are using the *conclusion* of the Cosmological Argument (that God exists) in order to secure the validity of one of its premises (that all events have causes). Again a circular procedure. But of course if Mascall replies that *independently* of his theism he is still sure that all events have causes, then I cannot see what rational procedure could either confirm or falsify that claim.

Our argument over causality need not, however, be regarded as profitless. Many people who feel confident that 'Every event has a cause' is true and non-vacuous undoubtedly do so because they confuse it with statements about the success of scientific method, or deduce it from their prior belief in God's sovereignty. And our discussion should at least have shown these people the weakness of their position, when regarded as a foundation for the Cosmological Argument.

4

Suppose, however, we allowed that the universe might in fact demand a cause. Suppose we agree that it cannot 'owe its existence to itself', but must owe it to some other being. Would this concession be enough to rid the Argument of its difficulties?

Only if, for one thing, we could be sure that the being who caused the universe to exist did not himself require a cause of a still higher order. If everything without exception demands a cause, then God must have *his* cause too. God, replies the Thomist

[1] E. L. Mascall, *Christian Theology and Natural Science* (London: Longmans, Green and Co, 1956), pp. 200 f.

is the author of his own existence. But then, his critic can point out, here *is* an exception to the rule: not everything demands a cause, after all. And if this is so, how do I know that the *world* demands a cause, or everything in the world? Admit exceptions, and the Cosmological Argument at once loses its purchase.

The agnostic may begin to erect a plausible case for himself on these lines. (i) The Cosmological Argument concludes that there is one being who owes his existence to himself. (ii) Among the premises of the Argument is the claim that *no* being owes its existence to itself. Therefore. . . . The Thomist interrupts him, 'No *finite* being owes its existence to itself. But that does not rule out the possibility of an *infinite* being—an infinite being which may very well owe its existence to itself.'

Does this crush the agnostic's attempt to show that the Argument contradicts itself? Not entirely. For how is the Thomist to characterize this 'infinite being'? The phrase is by no means self-explanatory. In practice, when he does try to give an account of its meaning, he is forced to include among other attributes the attribute of owing existence to itself. That is to say, the appeal to 'infinite being' is not an *answer* to the problem that the agnostic raised; but merely substitutes for the originally puzzling idea another idea in which the first is covertly contained. 'Infinite being' cannot be unpacked without reference to 'author of own existence'.

This difficulty might be nicknamed the problem of halting the regress of causes. If for the moment we assume that the regress *could* be halted at the point where the argument requires it to halt, a new difficulty at once arises, a peculiarly *religious* difficulty.

The God at whom we would have arrived by tracing back the causal regress would be a God far too closely tied to his creation to satisfy Christian demands for his 'otherness' or transcendence. Whatever inaugurated the causal sequence would be part and parcel of the natural world in which it is causally operative. We may think we can conceive of an alternative, but only through a tempting sleight of imagination. Why *not* imagine a being entirely outside the universe, infusing energy *into* the universe, without becoming in any way part of it? Why is this absurd? It is absurd because in imagining this, we inevitably picture the world as a limited system with a boundary beyond which dwells the God who is the world's cause. But this would really be no different from thinking of a *part* of the world and of a being who dwells in *another* part but is in contact with the first. Paul Tillich is perfectly right when he says that the Cosmological Argument degrades God to the level of the world itself.[1] Alternatively, we could say, to be an adequate object of worship, God must be wholly independent of the world. But the Cosmological Argument finds a place for God as the one who completes the world's pattern: he is the missing piece of the cosmic jig-saw—a crucial piece no doubt, but not so utterly different from all the other pieces as piety requires him to be.

5

A page or two back I touched lightly on a vexing problem, the problem of what sense we can make of statements that talk about 'the whole universe'. When we are seriously speaking of absolutely everything there is, are we speaking of something that requires a cause, in the way that events *in* the universe may require causes? What indeed can be safely said at all about the totality of things? For a great many remarks that one can make with perfect propriety about limited things quite obviously can*not* be made about the cosmos itself. It cannot, for instance, be said meaningfully to be 'above' or 'below' anything, although things-in-the-universe can be so related to one another. Whatever we might claim to be '*below* the universe' would turn out to be just some more *universe*. We should have been relating part to part, instead of relating the whole to something not-the-universe. The same

[1] *Systematic Theology*, Vol. I (Chicago: University of Chicago Press, 1951), p. 205.

applies to 'outside the universe'. We can readily imagine a boundary, a garden wall, shall we say, round something that we want to call the universe. But if we imagine ourselves boring a hole through that wall and pushing a stick out *beyond* it into a nameless zone 'outside', we should still not in fact have given meaning to the phrase 'outside the universe'. For the place into which the stick was intruding would deserve to be called a part of the universe (even if consisting of empty space, no matter) just as much as the area within the walls. We should have demonstrated *not* that the universe has an outside, but that what we took to be the whole universe was not really the whole.

Our problem is .this. Supposing we could draw up a list of questions that can be asked about objects in the universe, but cannot be asked about the *whole* universe: would the question, 'Has it a cause?' be on that list? One thing is clear. Whether or not this question is on the proscribed list, we are not entitled to argue as the Cosmological Argument does that *because* things in the world have causes, therefore the sum of things must also have *its* cause. No more (as we have just seen) can we argue from the fact that things in the world have tops and bottoms, insides and outsides, and are related to other things, to the belief that the universe has *its* top and bottom, inside and outside, and is related to a supra-cosmical something.

Neo-Thomists themselves are sometimes aware of the logical trickiness of talk about the totality of things. In the book quoted earlier, Dr Mascall casts doubt on claims that the second law of thermodynamics can properly be said to apply to the world as a whole, to produce a theory of a 'running-down universe'.[1] It is most dubious whether we can attribute to the universe either a 'boundary' or an 'environment'; and it cannot therefore be considered as on all fours with the closed, 'lagged' systems from the study of which the relevant laws were formulated. Should he not be equally unsure whether the notion of *cause and effect* can be transposed from the description of limited events to a cosmic

[1] *Op. cit.*, p. 142.

setting? John Laird's suspicion seems justified—that while the world is indeed the *theatre* of causes and effects, we are not entitled to claim that it is itself an effect of some super-cause.[1] I cannot be dogmatic here; for I am not able to discover any clear principles on which to construct the list of things that one can and cannot, sensibly, say about the universe as a whole. The fact of this uncertainty, however, is quite enough to refute the scholastic's claim that the Cosmological Argument is logically foolproof and affords sure knowledge of God. The believer who builds his faith on it is taking a big gamble in logic. Yet this is *not* how his situation is presented to him by the Catholic apologist.

The universe is not a limited thing like a box of biscuits or a galaxy. More helpfully; the word 'universe' is not a thing-word. and therefore it must not be expected to conform to the logical behaviour of thing-words. Popular apologists often present the Argument in terms of our inability to say of any given being, nebula or single atom, 'This just brought itself into being.' Suppose that nebula or atom were the sole and original occupant of the universe, it would, they argue, require a cause, some impetus from without. But we can reject this and any similar version of the Argument by refusing to identify the nebula or atom or whatever it is with *the universe*. To identify them is to forget the lesson just learned, that thing-words and words like 'cosmos' and 'universe' have crucially different logics. Indeed, the farther science moves from the Newtonian picture of the world (matter disposed about a space-receptacle), the larger the gulf between their logics seems to become.

Those points have widely ranging application in neo-scholastic writings. Even when not formally employing the Cosmological Argument, these writers frequently speak of God as the one who 'sustains', 'conserves', 'energizes', 'maintains' the cosmos in being. These words are innocent-looking, respectably scientific in appearance. But in these contexts they are not doing a scientific

[1] See Professor John Laird, *Theism and Cosmology* (London: Allen and Unwin, 1940), p. 95.

job. Here lies the danger of their use. A scientist may 'energize' a circuit in an experimental situation; and we know what he means by that. He may 'maintain' a gas at a constant temperature and pressure; and *that* is intelligible enough. But once more transplant those words from these contexts, and speak of energizing and maintaining *the universe*; and although an impression of intact meaning remains (plus the 'prestige' overtones of scientific jargon), yet no firm meaning may actually be left. So great is the difference between a limited electric circuit, a gas in a flask, and—the sum of things.[1]

[1] I made a number of these points in a review of *Christian Theology and Natural Science* in *The Journal of Theological Studies*, Vol. VIII, Part 2, pp. 385 ff.

CHAPTER TEN
GOD AND COSMOS (2)

—————

I

NOT every version of the Cosmological Argument turns on the notions of cause and effect. St Thomas's Third Way— the argument about 'might-not-have-beens'—uses instead the concepts of 'contingency' and 'necessity'. The contingent is what happens to exist, but need not have existed: necessary being is being that *has* to exist, that cannot *not* exist. The argument states that if there are contingent beings, there must be a necessary being. The one is correlative to the other, like 'front' and 'back', 'up' and 'down', 'convex' and 'concave'. The fact of a contingent world implies the fact of a necessary being whose world it is, and whose permanence stands behind the world's mutability.

The first difficulty about this version arises from the fact that 'necessary' and 'contingent', when used as correlatives, are words normally at home in speaking not of things or beings, but of propositions; a 'necessary' proposition being one that cannot be denied without contradition, whereas a contingent one can. If we wish to keep this logical use of 'necessary' and 'contingent', we could rephrase the Argument in this way: 'The proposition "God exists" is necessary.' That is, it would be contradictory to deny God's existence. But Hume very properly objected to this that one may deny the existence of any thing or person whatever and never involve oneself in logical contradiction, although sometimes, of course, in falsity. To get a contradiction in such a sentence, one would have to include in the *concept* of whatever being one was considering the idea of its existence. Only then would the denial of its existence contradict what had already been said. Before 'existence' *could* be part of the concept of any being, it would have to be looked on as a characteristic or attribute of that being—like its colour or size or personality. But there are good logical reasons for saying that 'existence' is *not* a word that stands for a characteristic, that it *cannot* stand as part of the minimum description of any being. Once all the describing is *complete*, one may then add, 'And there *is* such a being'; or, 'It doesn't exist really.' But to say this is not to go on listing new characteristics: it is to do something quite different.

To sum this up: if the Argument demands a regress from beings whose non-existence is conceivable to a being whose non-existence is *in*conceivable, then it fails. There can be no such regress, for its terminus would be not only infinitely remote but also logically impossible.

This is what happens when we interpret the word 'necessary' as referring to our way of asserting God's existence; namely, when we take his existence as logically necessary. One might try, however, to avoid this impasse by taking it in a different way, as saying something about God's mode of existence itself. To call his existence 'necessary' might be to express its 'complete actuality, indestructibility . . . independence of limiting conditions'.[1] But would this help? Not really: for these and the like characteristics now refer once again to the questions of *causality* that we have already found so perplexing. To call God completely actual and independent of conditions are ways of stating that he is the being who causes all things, but owes his existence to nothing, and cannot forfeit his existence through the action of any other being. Part of the elusiveness of the whole Argument comes from this oscillation between logical and causal senses of 'necessary'. It can easily be brought out by considering the clearly ambiguous sentence, 'God necessitates himself'. If this is taken as *causal*

[1] A. C. A. Rainer, in *New Essays in Philosophical Theology*, p. 68.

necessitation, then the version of the Cosmological Argument to which the sentence leads back is plainly a causal version, and exposed to the criticisms already made. If it is *logical* necessitation, then the sentence is equivalent to ' "God exists" is logically necessary', a claim that we have just seen to be untenable.

These are the main objections currently made again the Argument by linguistic philosophers. It is worth adding that were these objections in every case unfounded and the Argument sound, what it actually would have established is very much less remarkable than many apologists imply. Following Kant, we could argue that we make good sense of the idea of necessity, when we are told of the conditions under which whatever is necessary *is* necessary. Given such and such conditions, then such and such is necessarily the case. But the notion of God, we are told, is of an *'unconditionally* necessary' being. And this phrase, although *grammatically* unimpeachable, is logically vacuous; rather like 'surfaceless sphere', and not far from 'non-canine dog'. Secondly, if the causal versions of the Argument are effective, they establish that one being exists, which causes the world but is not itself caused. This *negative* part of the conclusion ('a being which is not itself caused') is constantly transformed in an illicit way into the *positive* assertion that God (now taken as the full theist or Christian God) is the 'Author of his own being', that he 'bestows being upon himself and upon the world'. Here we have clearly and obviously personal characteristics being conjured out of the mere fact (if fact it be) that the cause of the world can*not* be said to have a cause. God *may* be personal: but we cannot learn that by verbal acrobatics like these.

Those criticisms do not apply to certain scholastics who do admit the meagreness of the conclusions derived from the Argument. A number of them see it as doing no more than pointing the way to a mystery that only *revelation* can penetrate; as a preparation for receiving knowledge about God from quite another source. This is admirable caution. But on the other hand, if the Argument is logically invalid, it may not be able to fulfil even those humble functions.

2

The current objections to the Cosmological Argument are, I think, fairly decisive refutations of its most frequently used forms. There are, however, other refinements, sophisticated restatements of the Argument, which are claimed by those who use them to escape the criticisms of Hume, Kant, and the modern analysts.

The scholastic may agree that if God is thought of as the First Cause or Mover in the *ordinary* sense of 'cause' and 'move', then he *would* be merely an item in the regress of causes and movers and therefore of a piece with the world. But, he will continue, these words are not being used in the Argument in quite their normal senses. God does not 'move' the world as my hand moves my pen: he does not preserve it as a librarian preserves an ancient manuscript, or sustain it as a patron sustains an artist—nor is he related to the world in *any* of the ways in which one finite thing is related to any other finite thing, not even as cause is related to effect. Between God and cosmos exists a quite unique 'cosmological relation'—of which nothing *in* the world provides an instance, although many things in the world provide *analogies*.[1] These analogies 'sharpen our sense for the uniqueness of this [relation]'. 'Causality . . . is simply an analogy, which points beyond itself to the inexpressible fact of creation.' [2] The Argument *would* collapse into absurdity, if 'causality' were taken *literally* as the relation of God to world. It *must* not be so taken: therefore the Argument may not collapse.

This move cannot be censured as a mere retreat to obscurant-

[1] See Austin Farrer, *Finite and Infinite* (London: Dacre Press, 1943), *passim.*

[2] Farrer, *op. cit.*, pp. 285, 269.

ism. In view of the kind of criticisms I have been using against
simpler versions of the Argument, I am in no position to deny
that if it is at all meaningful to speak of a relation between the
world and God, that relation cannot be an instance of relations
we encounter in our dealings with finite beings. If it *were*, God
would be made a creature among creatures. The analogical version seems at once to strengthen and to weaken the Argument. It
strengthens it against logical criticism by passing beyond any
rigorous, formal, syllogistic pattern of reasoning, into the realm
of unanalysable, only half-communicable, movements of thought.
It weakens it through moving away from its original empirical
basis. What we 'discover' in our environment are countless instances of event causing event, in the *ordinary*, everyday sense of
'cause'. And so the idea of a regress of causes, moving to the
limits of our experience and beyond, is a plausible and powerful
one. The same is *not* true of the quite unique 'cosmological relation' that is now to replace the familiar causal relation. What the
regress of causes supposedly demanded is always another of the
same, another *cause*, and nothing in the world seemed capable of
halting that regress: hence God. But now God is introduced *not*
in response to the demand for an ultimate cause, but as standing
to the world in a relation only faintly *analogous* to that of cause
to effect. But if this is so, is it plausible to say any longer that the
regress of causes *drives us on* to posit God, as it certainly seemed
to do in the unsophisticated versions of the Argument, and as it
has to do for the Argument to gain momentum enough to carry
itself out of our experience altogether?

We appear to be checked either way. The Argument has most
drive if we interpret it naïvely as requiring God as 'cause' in the
ordinary sense. But this makes him *less* than God. If we think
more adequately of God's relation to the world, it becomes far
less obvious that the world *demands* such a being, so related to it.
It certainly no longer follows from the facts of cause and of
movement observed within the world.

Further, so long as we thought of God as standing to the

world as its cause, we could readily agree that such a being might well explain the world's existence, just as certain finite events can explain other finite events that stand to them in the same relation. But if we are to talk, instead, of a unique cosmological relation between God and world, not causality as we know it, then it is not so certain that to claim that God stands to the cosmos in this *peculiar* relation is to explain anything. It becomes, to say the least, exceedingly hard to decide whether we are being offered an explanation of a very queer sort, or no explanation at all.

3

What is hardest of all to decide (and my discussion of this must be somewhat inconclusive) is whether or not there *is* such a relation as the sophisticated versions speak of, or how we could decide whether there is or not. Are they gesturing towards, stammering about, some real but scarcely expressible relation, or are they creating the illusion of one only? We might recall here Professor Flew's suspicion that Christians appear to make bold assertions about God, but whittle those claims away by successive qualifications, until the original assertion is left vacuous—although *looking* as momentous as ever. Could the same be happening here? The cosmos is related to a being, but *not* as effect is related to cause, nor quite as design to designer, artefact to artist, nor . . . nor. . . . How could we tell whether anything meaningful survives this process of erosion? It does not, superficially, look as if any meaning *could* survive. No *specific* relation known to us, nor *combination* of relations, will be accepted by the theologian as being his target: we know this in advance. We may simply reach an impasse in which the objector says, 'Well, there's no room left for any relation at all'; and the defender says, 'If you can't see it, you can't see it. But, to me, all these analogies point to a relation that is mysterious but real.'

Two examples may clarify the situation: perhaps neither of

them exactly describes that situation, but they may give us a new bearing on it. First, we are given a map-reference to a road junction. The junction lies *not* on the top edge of the map, *nor* on the left edge of the map, but at a given, determinate distance from each. With this information, we can easily locate it. Second, suppose we are told that the road junction lies in a determinate direction from a church and in another direction from a hilltop. But we are not told what these compass directions are. We ask, is it due north of the church, 10° east of the hill? and so on. But the answer we receive to each question is, no: no matter what compass direction we suggest. In this case we cannot obtain a 'fix' on the junction; or even have adequate reason to believe in its existence, save by hearsay. It is absolutely no help to be told that nevertheless the church and the hilltop do give clues to its location.

In the theological case, God is said to be related to the world; and clues to the nature of that relation are to be found in cause-effect, artist-artefact relations, but in neither of these absolutely, nor in any *other* dependence-relation. And, most important, no accurate specification can be given of the logical direction from these in which the one correct relation can be discovered. (This is the force of calling that relation 'inexpressible'.) The lack of such specification is what makes this case suspiciously like the second example. Putting the point as sympathetically as possible: we need great caution in accepting an argument that runs so acute a risk of speaking of a 'relation' that may be no relation at all. The ordinary senses of 'cause', 'create' etc. yield nonsense and heresy, when applied to God's relation with the world. Thus, these are amended, in ways that cannot be *in principle* accurately specified (no compass bearing), in order to do justice to the cosmological relation in all its uniqueness. But it is apparent that we cannot consider so precarious an argument as this as a 'certain' demonstration of a God who stands in the cosmological relation to the world: at the most, this conclusion would be a bold surmise.

We should be more optimistic if we could fall back on a knowledge by acquaintance of God, and of the relation between him and the world. To illustrate this, suppose we are looking at a landscape from a hillside, trying to identify a particular farmhouse. We have been living there, and thus are acquainted with its appearance. In this case, a most *un*-specific direction hint could be enough to bring my gaze to the relevant sector of my view, and then without further help I might spot the house. In the same way, if we had independent knowledge of God (and hence of the cosmological relation), we should manage to identify it from the various directions given by the theologian, such as they are. But this would be much more than a variation of the argument we have been reviewing. It would introduce new premiss-material, of a controversial kind: in fact, it re-introduces the claims to encounter with God discussed in Chapters Three and Four. The Cosmological Argument would, further, have lost that neat, brief, formal structure that commends it so much to the apologist.

But if in the end I am sceptical about the Argument, my scepticism takes the form of a genuine suspension of judgement, rather than a hostile dogmatism. I *do* seem able to attach something rather *like* good sense to the notion of a Ground for the world's existence, that is not strictly its cause or its designer . . . especially when the vision of such a being is expressed through the medium of great poetry. But it seems to me equally possible that this is ultimately a misleading and deluding vision, produced by subtle amalgamation of the various analogical elements—'cause', 'designer', 'Father', etc. into a highly solemn composite image. This image might be unique in its impressiveness, but still not provide a logically satisfactory account of a universe related to a supramundane being, nor give grounds for believing that such a being must exist.

4

Apologists employ a large variety of auxiliary arguments and re-flections in order to reinforce the Cosmological Argument proper. We have seen how that argument attempts to create a sense of de-pendence—of thing depending upon thing, of world depending upon God. So too the auxiliaries are chiefly concerned to heighten a sense of the precariousness of all finite existence; a sense of in-stability that can be countered only by the belief that underneath are the everlasting arms. Or, if there are *no* everlasting arms, if there is no upholder, then there is nothing but vertigo, meaning-lessness, and despair.

So scholastics speak of the striving of our thought and aspira-tion towards the infinite, the 'natural drive of the mind towards transcendence, which must be seen in close connexion with the will's drive towards the infinite good'.[1] This is not yet *argument*, but easily *acquires* apologetic force, as St Thomas's use of it clearly has in the following sentence. 'This orientation of mind to the infinite would be in vain, unless there were an infinite in-telligible thing, which must be the supreme being, and this we call God.'[2]

I see two main obstacles to agreeing with St Thomas. The first one is that there seems nothing logically impossible in human beings setting themselves infinitely distant goals of aspiration; even although they might prove unrealizable in full, and even although there existed no perfect being who either realized them in his own person or who set those goals before humanity. To be able to pursue perfection does not entail that perfection exists; any more than the procession of natural numbers demands that there exists some last and greatest number of all.

[1] Fr. F. C. Copleston, *Aquinas* (Harmondsworth: Pelican Books, 1955), p. 248.
[2] *Ibid.*, p. 249, quoting St Thomas, *Summa Contra Gentiles*, I, 43.

A second difficulty arises from the meaning of 'this . . . would be vain, unless . . .'. This phrase contains an important presupposition, namely that nothing in the world can be expected to be 'vain', irrational, or unplanned. But the only satisfactory guarantee that the world was like this would be the belief that it is a world planned by an omnipotent, benevolent, all-wise deity. So it does not look as if it were possible to know in advance of experience that every detail of the world is rationally planned, without assuming at the start what this argument would like to reach as its conclusion. The atheistic-romantic conception of man as ceaselessly striving for an ultimately unattainable, but infinitely desirable goal, is not, therefore, a self-demolishing one, as St Thomas's language would imply. If the world is not *completely* rational, coherent; and if we cannot make *perfect* sense of it, that is not to deny that it is rational and coherent *to a degree*, or that quite an amount of sense can be made of some of it—enough for the maintenance of sanity, the setting before us of practical objectives, and even the radical manipulation of nature which is applied science.

That last sentence sums up my reply to a recent article by a Catholic writer, Brother Leo Williams. The Cosmological Argument asserts the necessity of God's existence. Well, says Brother Williams, that means that it is impossible to deny his existence. Why impossible? Questions of logical necessity are not, he thinks, crucial here. It is impossible (for him at least) to deny God's existence, because the implications of atheism are so unthinkably grim. This would be the world of Hardy's novel, where 'the President of the Immortals had finished his sport with Tess': a world of no purpose, with no explanation. 'It is as unbearable as that.' But, scientists and people in everyday life do make sense of the situation in which they live and of problems with which they contend. We must assume that there *is* purpose, explanation, sense. We do not live as if atheism were true. 'If nature was as heartless and witless as all that [as atheism requires it to be], why should it ever have come to be?' 'If everything in the end was to be frustration, the sceptic could have no interest in publishing his own scepticism.'[1]

In commenting on this, we must first of all think away as rhetorical extravagance the hint of Satanism brought by the Hardy reference, and by words like 'heartless' and 'witless' applied to nature. If nature is ultimately purposeless in some sense, that does not mean that it is dominated by an *evil* purpose. If there is to be no purpose, then let us take this quite seriously and not topple over from belief in benign deities to belief in malevolent ones, ignoring the middle possibility that there is no deity at all. But the more moderate claims made here are also challengeable. For one thing, we may again ask, 'Can *no* explanations be valuable unless *complete* and *ultimate* explanation is also possible?' In point of fact, we use the word 'explain' far more often to refer to *proximate* explanations than to ultimate ones. And it has been pointed out that the more sophisticated versions of the Cosmological Argument present us with a God related to the world in so peculiar a way that it is not in the least certain that his existence does explain the world in any intelligible sense. The *absence* of such a being and the impossibility of such 'explanation' would not make our everyday or scientific explanation any less useful or reliable.

Similarly, it may in one sense be true that 'everything in the end [will] be frustration', if by that we mean that humanity will sooner or later (perhaps very *much* later) become extinct, and if there is no hereafter. But why should it follow from this that 'the sceptic could have no interest in publishing his own scepticism'? What is so absurd about a mortal and finite intelligent being concerning himself with inquiries into truth while he is able to do so, and believes these inquiries are as rewarding as any alternative pursuit he could engage in? On the other view, I might as well refuse to play with my dog (or even look after him) because he will be dead in the next year or two; or pay no heed to a piece of music because in ten minutes time it will have ended.

[1] Reviewing *New Essays in Philosophical Theology*, in *The Downside Review*, Summer 1956.

Earlier in this discussion, in talking of causality, I made the point that nature might be quite orderly enough to make science possible, even though certain events were 'uncaused'. In the same way, even although 'ultimate' explanations were unattainable, even though the universe is not transparent to the thought of any rational being, nor the manifestations of a single purpose, divine or otherwise, still the nightmare of Brother Williams would not be brought upon us. But only if it *were* brought upon us, would we be entitled to say, as he does say, that God's existence is *necessary*.

5

The precariousness of existence without God, I said, was what these auxiliary arguments seek above all to emphasize and make vivid. Obviously there are many ways of doing this, some of them logically impeccable. Others, like those just discussed, do rely upon faulty reasoning. One more specimen may usefully be added. It is an argument about *time*; and it comes from a book by Dom Illtyd Trethowan.

> That I should be constantly slipping away from reality . . . that my actions of five minutes ago should be (as it were) *dead*, and my life confined to the evanescent point which I call the present—this produces in me a spiritual vertigo if I cannot lay hold of an eternal somewhat to save the world from absurdity, from utter unreality.[1]

What is happening here is that the ordinary senses of the word 'present' have been quietly replaced by a new and artificially narrow sense. What 'I call the present' is normally *not* an 'evanescent point', despite Trethowan's assumption that it is. I speak (according to the context) of 'the present century', 'the present govern-

[1] Dom Illtyd Trethowan, *An Essay in Christian Philosophy* (London: Longmans, Green and Co, 1954), p. 67.

ment', of 'making the most of the present' (a holiday, a course of study, a romance). To expect that there should be, distinct from all these most flexible and proper uses, some one philosophically correct concept of 'The Present', is to fall victim to an abstracting vice that has received just castigation from a variety of recent philosophers.

Trethowan induces vertigo by suggesting that the sense of 'present' which it is alone proper for us to employ is that occasionally (rarely) needed one, in which the present is the slimmest of ridges between past and future. Both past and future are out of our reach. I cannot act *in* the future; and the past, we are told, even the most recent past, is '*dead*'.

One again, here is rhetorical extravagance posing as argument. To call the past 'dead' is to suggest, quite falsely, that all my memories (even of what I did five minutes ago) are as cold, remote, inaccessible, as my half-memory of a scarcely known great-aunt whom I have not seen for decades. What we properly call being '*alive*' is a process of acting, thinking, talking in a present which, as it were, draws its point, purpose, and sense largely from the past. The person who is most *intensely* alive is he whose words and actions spring from a deeply felt sense of the pattern of his life up to the present moment. His past is anything but 'dead' to him. It makes a continual impact upon the present.

Even if no 'eternal somewhat' undergirded our temporal existence, Trethowan's nightmare need not descend upon us, any more than Brother Williams's. Admittedly, the unbeliever must agree that if *he* does not reckon with his own past creatively, if he does not by his own efforts impose some sort of sense or shape on it, no one else can be counted upon to do it on his behalf. But that does not mean that the world lapses into 'absurdity' or 'utter unreality'. The sceptic has no obligation to commit spiritual suicide.

One does not have to believe that philosophical arguments must be either cogent and successful or else a worthless tissue of conceptual confusions. The arguments we have looked at in these two chapters are of very dubious validity, and yet their very persistence over the centuries, their deep psychological appeal to many of us, compel one to realize that they also express something of permanent human importance, whatever it is.

What is expressed seems to me to have two principal facets—the expression of *wonderment* and the expression of *anxiety*, both directed to highly general features of our experience. In the first case the Argument embodies the experience of wonder at the fact of there being a world at all: it is a movement of thought away from taking the world for granted; a shifting of attention from the nature, function, and uses of things to the simple but remarkable fact of their existence.

From another point of view the Argument expresses what can be called (solemnly) 'ontological anxiety', the anxiety inseparable from our situation as finite beings, vulnerable to all kinds of accidents and ailments, vulnerable above all to death: beings whose aspirations and yearning very often exceed their capacity to satisfy them. We may imagine a mode of being that is instead stable and invulnerable, where there is 'world enough and time' to accomplish our aims. The Argument indeed believes it can do more and can show that one being does really possess all these blessings and can bestow them on us. But it is here that we part company with its reasoning.

Paul Tillich's analysis of the Argument is wholly in accord with the tenor of this discussion. To him, the Cosmological Argument expresses our lack of self-sufficiency, but fails to prove that there exists a God who is all-sufficient and underivative. To talk of 'necessary existence' reminds us dramatically of *our* finitude and dependence; does not prove that any being *does* exist necessarily. 'The arguments for the existence of God neither are arguments nor are they proof of the existence of God. They are expressions of the *question* of God which is implied in human finitude.'[1]

We are entirely right to feel that the Kantian, Humean, and linguistic critiques of the Argument leave something important unsaid. But what they do not adequately deal with are not *logical* issues but those deep non-intellectual elements of wonderment and anxiety that seek expression in all of the many variant forms of cosmological reasoning. By themselves, however, they cannot repair the logical defects. In a world that no God had made, we could still wonder at the fact of its existence and ours. There might very well be less to wonder at than in the theist's world: but *this* fact would not be changed. In a godless world too, we should be perfectly able to experience ontological anxiety; but there is no sure path of inference from the presence of anxiety to the necessary existence of a comforter.

[1] *Systematic Theology*, Vol. I, p. 205.

CHAPTER ELEVEN

SCEPTICISM AND THE NATURALLY RELIGIOUS MIND

I

T HE starting-point of our whole study was the familiar fact
that religious language is a language of paradox. Some of
the paradoxes lie open to the view of every user or observer of
religious discourse. We work out our salvation with fear and
trembling, but it is *God* that works in us. God is *one* God; but a
unity-*in-Trinity*. He is closer than breathing; but he is in no
place. We pray to him *today*; but he is *outside time*. Other paradoxes unfold themselves fully only if the concept of God is sub-
mitted to logical analysis. But at whatever level they appear, the
pervasiveness of paradox cannot be denied.

We have not attempted to *reconcile* the paradoxes in this study.
We have taken a different approach, namely to inquire whether
there are ways open to us whereby we may accept the paradoxes
if we have to do so, but without abandoning belief. Two ways of
doing this suggested themselves to us. The first was the way of
ostensive definition: if God can be singled out, identified, what
matters it though our talk about him stammers in paradoxes? The
second way was the way of taking 'God' as an *explanatory* concept, and to that extent a meaningful concept, justifying its place
in the language, although still enigmatic in numerous other
respects.

Our results have been negative. We have found neither logically reliable procedures for identifying God nor for invoking him

as the explanation of features of the world or of the world's existence. But two things need to be said about those negative results. They cannot be taken as having by themselves shown a general or comprehensive breakdown in the logic of apologetics. For the problems and treatments of problems discussed in these pages have been only a very few out of those we *could* have selected. One glaring case of this selectivity is our brief discussion of the problem of miracle, a subject that is tackled very differently by different writers, and which we had room for here only as propounded by a single apologist. This is the price to be paid for deciding that analysis should turn to what theologians are actually saying and writing, in detail, rather than content itself with examining theological language *in vacuo*. A price, I think, that is well worth paying.

If these results are negative, they nonetheless carry important positive implications. It should have been made clear that no theology can ultimately escape those questions of meaning and verification with which we have been concerned—even those theologies which set their faces against natural religion, arguments for God's existence, or apologetics *in toto*. In so far as they use words at all, questions about the *use* of those words can and must be asked. And if the theologian accepts the linguistic philosopher's challenge, he need not see the ensuing discussion as merely a polemical skirmish against a fundamentally hostile mode of thinking. He may use the analyst's insights into the workings of language as a valuable instrument for helping him to clarify the logical structure of his own theology. We have repeatedly seen how much need there is for this sort of logical spring-cleaning within theology at the present time. We have seen the ambiguities between 'strict' and 'free' Christological theories, for instance; the uncertain fumbling over the analysis of personal encounters; tangled reasoning over the justification of moral decisions. In each of these areas of theological argument, and in many more, logical analysis is urgently required; and required in enormously greater detail than has been possible in a single survey like this.

I have admitted that we cannot argue from a selective set of studies to any general conclusion about the state of theology today. Yet enough may have been done to suggest that there is at least the *danger* that a breakdown in theology is taking place, despite the immense amount of self-assured talk of a contemporary 'theological renaissance'. No joyous casting aside of rational theology, as some Protestants are casting it aside, can dismiss the agonizing problems of sense and reference that confront even a 'revealed' religion. Now for the remainder of the book I am going to *suppose* that this radical breakdown has in fact taken place: and I am going to ask how we could most rationally and most imaginatively cope with it.

Is there, first of all, any way in which the Christian could frankly accept the situation with complete intellectual honesty but *without* the sacrifice of his faith? Could he hold his faith in such a way as to accommodate the loss of apologetic arguments, the ambiguities in religious experience, the failure of religious explanations and ostensive definitions? I believe he could; although only by a series of very daring (some will say wild) manœuvres.[1]

He may point out that as far as explanation is concerned, a great many believers have quite plainly given it little place in their thought. God has been held to be perfectly righteous, *in spite of*, not *because of*, the moral and immoral features of the world we live in. His goodness has not been appealed to as the *explanation* of the world's condition, which is a far from perfect one. Similarly, belief in God's perfect wisdom has not been taken as required by the design and purpose evidenced in nature. For there is also *im*perfection there and apparent purposelessness. Above all, he can say, the confident way in which an ardent believer holds his faith

[1] In what follows, I am drawing (in a most simplified form) upon Alasdair MacIntyre's essay in *Metaphysical Beliefs* (London: S.C.M., 1957).

is *not* the tentative and provisional way that is fitting for an explanatory hypothesis, always open to revision as a result of new evidence, and always liable to falsification. If you ask a thoughtful believer why he maintains his beliefs in a world that seems at every point to conflict with them, what he should say is that he accepts these beliefs *on the authority of Jesus*. Whatever the conceptual difficulties involved in speaking of God, we are provided by Jesus with sufficient information about Him—in language we can all understand—to be able to temper our agnosticism and enter upon an intelligible programme of worship and practical Christian living. This is a Christological theory, with the emphasis placed not on 'constructing' talk about God out of talk about Jesus, but on the testimony of Jesus to a God about whom we remain metaphysically ignorant, the enigmas in whose nature we do not resolve, and whose existence and attributes we make no move to verify. We walk by faith and not by sight. We are not argued into belief by the apologists, but converted by the impact of Jesus upon us into accepting his authority as absolute.

I do not think that this position can be attacked on purely logical grounds, if one should want to attack it. The Christian who adopts it abandons reliance on all the attempted 'justifications' and 'confirmations' of his faith that theologians have tried to produce. He stakes all upon the words and deeds of one man. of whose existence we learn through documents in which biography and interpretation are inextricably, or nearly inextricably, intertwined. He stakes all on this man, because here he is sure he has discovered that 'point in the world at which we worship [and] accept the lordship of something not ourselves'.[1] What forces him to his knees is not this or that bit of historical detective-work concerning some miracle or prophecy, but the overall intense and unique impression of this person who speaks with unparalleled authority, who inspires at once dread, reverence, and love.

To appeal in this way to an unanalysable personal impact may, as I suspect, be a logically invulnerable procedure. It is not of

---

[1] MacIntyre, *op. cit.*, p. 202.

course beyond another sort of challenge—from quite a different source. Just as different biographies, or paintings, of the same man may present violently contrasting impressions of their subject, so two readers of the New Testament may come away from their study of Jesus with two strongly contrasted pictures of his person, and with varying estimates of his authority. Discussion of the theological position that we have been examining would take the form not of the search for flaws of argumentation, aberrations from that standard uses of words, but of the comparison of and judgement between rival imaginative responses to the total New Testament witness to Jesus. Are we bowing the knee where it ought *not* to be bowed? Is our picture of Jesus dependent, as it should be, on the New Testament alone, or is it borrowing from sentimental literary and pictorial embroiderings? Are we being selective in the words and incidents in the Gospels that we allow ourselves to linger over: do we hurry over hard sayings and situations where in fact Jesus does not honestly impress us at all, but only puzzles us or bewilders us?

We must leave this approach and its problems here, for they have quite obviously ceased to be problems of logical analysis.

3

Suppose, on the other hand, that the impact Jesus makes upon some of us is not as compelling as to warrant our unconditional surrender to his authority. Then our supreme question would become how to cope in our practical living without Christian belief, for an indefinite period, or perhaps permanently. If we are people of a naturally religious mind, we should want to know how much of a religious orientation of life could be salvaged and retained in an agnostic setting, how far we could still think of life as fundamentally, being worthwhile; how far religiously-toned experiences once valued by us would be now shut off from us, and how far they would be still available.

In trying to answer certain of these questions, I shall keep in mind another class of people who are in just as much need of answers to them as the sceptic. I mean the Christian believer who is anxious and perplexed at the theologies of paradox, and wonders uneasily whether some day he will be forced to rename them theologies of contradiction; or who perhaps fears that there may not after all be enough secure historical knowledge on which to build his faith in the Incarnation. So long as he believes that loss of faith would bring with it the loss of all sense of worthwhileness and point in life, and that it would forever shut him off from those religious experiences that he has held supremely valuable, he is most likely to sacrifice intellectual integrity and suppress his anxieties. The doubts, however, will continue to take their toll, draining away enthusiasm and zest in living out his faith, leading possibly to a harsh suspicion of free inquiry in general. If we *could* show that a great many religious attitudes and experiences can be retained with sincerity, and that religious symbols can continue to have an important part in the life of the sceptic, this would remove the intolerable strain of believing that the ultimate choice is between Christian faith or a life not worth living at all; it would provide, as it were, a safety-net for him. It would at the same time show those who are already non-believers that they need do no violence to their religious natures, and that much of what that nature desires, but *because* of its scepticism feels shut out from, can be restored in another way.

Earlier chapters of this book have already tried to answer certain of these problems—particularly the chapter on moral judgement. If those theologians are wrong who have said 'no moral seriousness without religious belief', then the sceptic's worst forebodings can quickly be dispelled. I have argued that we can (and logically *must* be able to) make ultimate moral decisions that cannot depend on what God has said, done, or is.[1] Whether he is happy about it or not, even the theological moralist himself must make such a judgement before he can call God unconditionally

[1] See above, p. 130 ff.

191

good. I have also argued that a secular moral theory is quite well able to accommodate the idea of human dignity, human wickedness, the meaningfulness of life, and that it does not need to make nonsense of human love.

We shall turn now, however, to more specifically religious ways of conceiving morality, and inquire how far certain of *these* are affected by breakdown in orthodox belief. A starting-point for this will be found in a fact to which I drew attention in discussing the problems of historicity.[1] In so far as a story or parable delineates a way of life that we judge to be valuable, it is not of paramount importance whether or not the story or parable is historically true. It can do its job equally well if fictitious; sometimes better.

What job *can* it do? Mainly that of backing up a bare moral rule with an imaginatively vivid instance of its being practised or neglected. In a parable at its best we may have not only an illustration of what the rule enjoins, but also in very little space some useful pointers to difficulties likely to *impede* our obedience to it, insight into the good effects of obeying, and maybe still other sorts of information about it—all in one story. The peculiar beauty or grace or loathsomeness of ways of life can be brought out and kept easily before the mind in such stories, far more effectively than by memorizing lists of maxims. They are most memorable and most imaginatively satisfying when bound together as incidents of one life-story, or as the events of one drama, poem, or novel, given their own aesthetic unity. They provide (what again the maxims fail to provide) a resting-place for meditation, and a standing test for the vitality and 'spirit' of one's own moral life, not merely of its conformity to the rules.

It is tempting and plausible to go much further and claim that the Old and New Testaments *as a whole* (and other religious documents) provide a single extended 'story' or 'myth' or set of symbols, depicting a pattern of life and giving just the same sort of

[1] See above, p. 102.

aids to keen self-knowledge, and stimulus to moral effort, as the parable proper gives.[1] The moral pattern of life is the fundamental thing: the story its vehicle.

Some of the theologians we looked at earlier come very near to saying this: in particular the language of 'existential history' makes exactly the same emphasis—on what moral challenge history has at the present moment, not on the objective-factual happenings of the past. But the existentialist historian, we saw, does not stop there. He would not be easy in his mind if you told him that the biblical story was entirely fictitious, an extended parable *simply*, having the sole function of confirming a manner of living. He, and the vast majority of theologians with him, would insist that the attitudes that the biblical story evokes in its reader are responses to beliefs about certain *facts*—however curious facts they are—that God made the world, for instance, that he sent his Son, and that the man who believes in him shall not perish. ... They would deny that these responses would be obtained equally strongly if the story were taken as fictitious parable. It would be unthinkable to them that in one real sense Christ *need not have died*: for on the view we are considering, the *story* of his death (whether true or not) would be enough to give backing to the Christlike way of life.

But the view is obviously an immensely attractive one to anybody who wants to be at once empiricist and religious. For it holds that the problems about the meaning of words like 'God', 'heaven', 'resurrection' are solved by showing the part these words play in delineating the practical way of life. If they have a use of this kind, then they have a meaning. But the *Christian* surely cannot acquiesce in limiting the purpose of talk about God to this fortifying of morality by parable. The language of 'transcendence', the thought of God as a personal being, wholly other to man, dwelling apart in majesty—this talk may well collapse into meaninglessness in the last analysis. And yet to sacrifice it seems

[1] Compare R. B. Braithwaite, *An Empiricist's View of the Nature of Religious Belief* (C.U.P., 1955).

at once to take one quite outside Christianity. (In saying that I do not feel guilty of making an arbitrary definition of what Christianity is.)[1]

In a similar vein, a writer recently suggested that a real source of bafflement about God is our tendency to conceive him as a cosmic artisan or engineer manipulating the world, just in the way we (sinfully) seek to dominate and manipulate our environment and one another. St John said, 'God is love', and so he is quite literally. He belongs to the moral world, not to the world of cosmology and impersonality. His commandments are nothing but the statement of the 'conditions in which we either do or do not encounter Love, the only Source of Life'. Religious disciplines are ways of sensitizing the believer, making that encounter more enduring, and increasing the areas of life over which love is sovereign.[2]

Once more we note the centrality of moral judgement in this account. On morality everything else hinges. But the consequence again is to disqualify the theory as an account of *historical Christianity*. For if it rescues God from being a debased celestial mechanic, it is only to deny that 'he' is any sort of being at all, and instead to transform 'him' into a relation, the relation of love between persons. The metaphor of love 'standing between' people suggests (but of course does not justify) the fancy of personifying that relation and calling it 'God'.

If I conclude, then, that an account of religion in terms of a moral way of life backed up by parable fails as a description of Christianity, I do *not* want to go on and say that we can therefore count it of no value. For I see in it one way of answering some of the religiously-minded sceptic's worries; and of answering them most satisfactorily. For this account does illuminate very clearly some of the most important formal features of

---

[1] Here I disagree with Professor Braithwaite, who argues that an account of religious language in terms of 'parable' *is* compatible with traditional Christianity.

[2] John Wren-Lewis, *The Philosophical Quarterly*, July, 1955.

any religious orientation of mind. And it goes far to suggest a way of retaining such an orientation, despite the theological breakdown.

We could describe as 'religious' any set of attitudes and beliefs that satisfies three conditions. First, the believer commits himself to a pattern of ethical behaviour. This way of life is simply decided for as an ultimate moral choice: empirical facts will be relevant to his choice, but he can *derive* his decision from no facts whatever, not even from commands of God, should he believe in a God. But (second) what will distinguish religious from moral language is that religious discourse provides a tightly cohering extended parable or myth that vividly expresses the way of life chosen, and inspires the believer to implement it in practice. Third, the parable and its associated pattern of behaviour legislate not for any *fraction* of the believer's life, but for every aspect of it. It commands his supreme loyalty and determines his total imaginative vision of nature and man. Yet the believer suffers no loss of freedom through submitting himself to his faith: for the foundation upon which all is based would be his own freely endorsed value judgements. Defined in this broad, formal way, a religious orientation of life would not necessarily include belief in a God, nor in the possibility of speculative philosophy.

In current usage, however, the words 'religious' and 'religion' do not refer to form alone, but normally say something also about *content*. It cannot be emphasized too often that although I am claiming that a sceptic can, if he wishes, fashion a way of looking at life that merits to some degree the title 'religious', I am not claiming that he can provide for himself adequate substitutes for prayer, say, or the peculiarly Christian antidotes for anxiety or fear, or the hopes which are warranted only on certain Christian assumptions about the destiny of the world. I shall suggest in the final part of this chapter that there are a few important kinds of religious experience (that is to say, part of the *content* of theistic belief) that the sceptic *may* find are still available to him, in as much as these do not depend upon belief about the world or its deities, but upon other things. We shall, however, look first in a little more detail at the task of giving a religious form or structure to the moral life.

4

There is no more characteristic theological activity than that of sifting away 'unworthy' conceptions of God. God is not blemished by moral imperfections like men; he is morally perfect. We can think still more worthily of him than that, however. For he cannot be merely one perfect being among other possible perfect beings. He must be the source of all perfection: call him not simply 'good' but 'goodness itself'. All else is unworthy of him. He is also lord of the universe, and so (as we have seen) cannot be thought of as just one item in the furniture of that universe. It must be inconceivable that he should *not* exist: he must exist necessarily. Or (moving in yet another direction), we think unworthily of him as long as we think of him as 'being' at all: he is beyond being.

Christians have made all these affirmations, searching for that notion of God which excludes all unworthy limitations. For while the least suspicion of unworthiness remains, it cannot be *God* that is being spoken about or prayed to: by definition, he is the one in whom there is no unworthiness at all.

But it must seem to many people, even to would-be believers, that if those refinements must be made, they elevate God not only out of imperfection, but also and equally out of personal existence of any kind. 'Goodness', like 'love', cannot be seriously personified without absurdity. Conclusions can follow necessarily from premisses, but nothing can *exist* necessarily. And if God is beyond being: is this not to agree with the atheist, who says 'There is no God'? If it is *not* the same, then we still await from the theologian a satisfactory account of the difference between his claim and that of the atheist.

Scepticism and the Naturally Religious Mind

The trend of this reasoning can be summed up in two ways. Either we say, 'God, to be God, must be non-existent: atheism is the purest form of faith.' Or else we can say (more wisely if less sensationally) that the 'only thoroughly satisfactory object of reverence, or focus of ideals, must be imaginary'.[1] I say more wisely, because to call this imaginary focus 'God' outright is to take the risk of allowing the incompatible Christian claims about God as 'personal', as 'active', and so on, to return, despite the judgement that on logical grounds they must be excluded.

Now what bearing do these reflections have upon our 'formal' account of religion as parable associated with a way of life? A very close bearing. The sceptic cannot conscientiously believe in God as the New Testament depicts him. It would seem to follow that little or nothing could be usefully salvaged by him from the concept of God. But we can see now that this is not wholly true. Our religiously minded sceptic can be seen as perpetually in quest of the most satisfactory set of parables to sum up his moral decisions. He will achieve progress, whenever he manages to replace some ambiguous, sprawling story by a terse illuminating one, or finds a more comprehensive symbol for a wide range of experiences he wishes to consider as related together in some way. His *ideal*, doubtless never to be realized, is to catch up his whole understanding of life as it is and as it should be in a single unified vision. The notion of an ideal imaginary focus is precisely what he needs in making clear to himself the nature of this task, and in pointing the direction in which his quest must go. And it is as a development of the idea of God that this notion is most readily derived.

He faces a many-sided task. It involves the scrutiny of alternative modes of living, seen as far as possible in the round, realized vividly in the imagination, and held in some powerful symbol. The field from which he will glean material is indefinitely large. It need not be confined to a single sacred book, nor indeed to

[1] Compare, in this section, Professor J. N. Findlay's article, 'Can God's Existence be Disproved?', in *New Essays in Philosophical Theology*.

o

explicitly theological writings. He may stock his armoury of symbols from such novels as Orwell's *Animal Farm*, and Koestler's *Darkness at Noon*; from Dostoievsky's *The Idiot*, from Bunyan and from Spenser, promiscuously; from Euripides in *The Bacchae*. Upon each encounter with these and the like myth-makers something will be taken, something rejected; the moral struggle seen more sharply through the lens of the new parable; new linkages made between old symbols—across the years, between the authors, and between the cultures. It is a task in which imagination cooperates intimately with moral judgement—discriminating, amending, adapting, in order to build up an image of the best way of life and of the best way of capturing it, in myth, parable, and symbol.

This still does not exhaust the field from which material may be taken. The richest store of all may, of course, be found in one's own personal experience of life, as retained by memory. By reflecting creatively on one's past, one may strive to draw together the strands of one's life into the total parable, bringing them into relation (the closest we can attain) with the ideal, unattainable focus.

To organize one's life in this way, would I think be admitted by some people as a genuinely religious activity, in one acceptable sense of the word. But others will be far more struck by the *difference* between it and traditional religions, and lament how bleak a prospect it extends to the unfortunate sceptic. It is a religion only of the *individual*, he will say—the working out of private myths in private ivory towers. Whereas, 'true' religion essentially involves fellowship, the breaking down of barriers, the sharing of *public* worship centred on a *public* parable. Or again, he may judge that the sceptic cuts a rather pathetic figure, once one sees what solid beliefs he is really left with. In a friendless, enormous universe, he makes his little decisions and clothes them in stories of his own devising, seeking to forget his puniness, his mortality, his loneliness, like a condemned prisoner scratching feeble drawings on the walls of his cell. Third, he may say, 'Call this view of life "religious" if you like, but does it really deserve the name, if you set alongside it (something it cannot duplicate) the great Christian theme of the soul's pilgrimage or adventure into the unknown, with faith as its sole guide?'

I think it can be shown that these three indictments, although natural enough, are not altogether fair.

First, we must admit that there is certainly no guarantee that any one set of symbols, any one parable, will commend itself to a sufficiently large number of people as to constitute a shared, public religion. But since the parables are desired above all to express a *moral* pattern of life, that is, to embody a blue print for social, not solitary living, it is to be expected that people who hold to similar moral patterns will also respond sympathetically to the same parables, that they should take seriously one another's criticisms of the *adequacy* of those parables, as people engaged in a common task.

Whatever the differences among their parables and symbols, secular religious people would be united in one respect. All would be engaged in the same sifting, discriminating activity that we have tried to describe earlier. But to stress *this*, it might be objected, would be rather like making a religion out of the *search* for a religion. It might be: but would that be so paradoxical, or even so very unfamiliar? Theologians constantly declare that no analogy or image or symbol can adequately express God's nature. He is Father, but not in all respects like earthly fathers; he loves us, but with more than a human love . . . and so on. The best that can be done is to assert some analogy and then say, 'But no: he is not quite like that', and then another analogy, and largely cancel it in turn. No shot is a bull's-eye, but the cluster of near-misses manages to locate the target in a rough-and-ready fashion. More seriously: the progress towards knowledge of God includes the destruction of successive symbols, the endless pruning away of misleading associations. The aim of all this labour (to the Christian) is a knowledge of a God who in some sense *is*. The sceptic, denying this, may nevertheless engage in his closely analogous search for parable—with a sense of equal dedication and of fellowship with others who undertake it along with him.

Second: the Christian's symbols and parables not only back up a set of moral decisions (the Christian ethic) but also tell him something about the world he lives in. The heavens declare God's glory: he makes the clouds his chariot and walks upon the wings of the wind. No corner of the universe lacks his presence. If we make our bed in hell, behold he is there. Personal being, intelligence, and purpose are to be encountered not only in humanity and in the works of humanity; but the entire world is replete with them. So far the Christian. Is he right in claiming that without these religious assumptions the world could be seen as little more than a vast friendless tomb or prison?

Our religiously minded sceptic would be entitled to reply that this grim vision is by no means *forced* upon sceptics. It is one out of many possible imaginative slants on the world, none of which is more authoritative than any other, so long as they all are consistent with the facts.[1] To take one very simple instance. Men certainly are minute compared in size and length of life with, say, the solar system. Yet anyone who concluded 'Men therefore are miserable creatures—tiny and pathetically short-lived' would be expressing only one (imaginatively interesting though chilly) slant, but not at all the whole truth. Someone else might properly reply, 'No; men are large creatures and long-lived: compare them with molecules and lightning flashes.'

To take another example: 'Nature is indifferent to all values: see her callousness in the T.B. bacillus and polio virus.' This invites the reply, 'But without these natural conditions, without *just* those evolutionary mechanisms, no intelligent life or purpose or awareness of beauty would have ever been possible.' Neither a satanic nor a benign vision exhausts nature's ambiguity. Poets and painters are endlessly singling out alternative pictures of man's relation to nature. Some are quixotic and fanciful, the play-

[1] See Antony Flew and Ronald W. Hepburn, 'Problems of Perspective', in *The Plain View* for Winter 1955.

thing of a lyric or sketch: but one lingers over others, because in some way they project on to nature a vision with which one would be well content to live, which one would choose, before any other perspective, as providing the perfect backcloth to the way of life one has opted to follow. If we set supreme value upon *men*, then the perspective will not be one in which men are dwarfed by cosmic immensity: the world will be seen as the theatre of moral drama; elements in nature as symbols of human conflicts, achievements, and disasters. We may, of course, realize from time to time that our slant is no more than one out of many other possible slants, and that it is sustained by the work of imagination. But we will be fortified by recalling that the alternative to the slant we seek to maintain (the one which backs up our moral decisions) is some *other* slant, which does this task less effectively. The alternative is not 'reality' in place of 'illusion'; for *every* way of looking at nature in the round involves plumping for some slant or other. There is no escaping them. Obviously then, the religiously minded sceptic will search not only for symbols that directly express his moral judgements in human terms (like the Grand Inquisitor in Dostoievsky, or Big Brother in *Nineteen Eighty-Four*), but at the same time for what we could call symbols of *context* or *setting* (like the nature poems of Kathleen Raine, or the landscapes of Graham Sutherland or Paul Nash).

In short, nature is pliant to the imagination to an extent often ignored by orthodox theologians: and sceptics are not necessarily immured within some single fearful dungeon of loneliness from which there can be no escape. On the other hand, it would be foolish to claim that an agnostic's imaginative slant, however well adapted to his judgements of value, could provide an exact equivalent to the biblical conceptions of God's presence in every part of the universe or of his love for man. To take a critical case: the Christian would deny that a man who suffered and perhaps died in complete solitariness was out of the reach of real personal encounter during his ordeal; the denial of this is part of what is meant by his talk of God's omnipresence. The unbeliever has no equivalent comfort, and would be unwise to delude himself that he had.

Third: the idea of life as 'pilgrimage' is an astonishingly pervasive one among religions of widely different types. It is at home most naturally among those that believe men to be capable of reaching beatitude in the strength of their own aspiring love for God. But even those forms of Christianity which most vigorously deny men the power to 'save themselves', and see salvation as God's work alone, have still clung to the pilgrimage-motif, and in fact developed it more richly than the other. If Plotinus sums up the first group with his quest of the alone to the Alone, Bunyan's Pilgrim nobly represents the second. It would be, on the face of it, quite reasonable to complain that if our secular religious orientation could not in any way embrace this notable image of pilgrimage, it would be very much poorer and less satisfying in consequence.

The sense of movement, voyaging, questing, in the Christian notion of pilgrimage, has (at least) two strands. First, there is the effort to realize the demands of Christian ethics, the 'movement' from challenge to challenge, the discovery of ways of coping with a succession of testing situations (Vanity Fair, the Slough of Despond), all of which are incorporated as significant landmarks in the pilgrimage-route. Next, as a kind of counterpoint to this theme, the pilgrimage is equally a journey 'from this world to that which is to come'.[1] The imagery of moral progress as a journey merges with that of death as a journey to the hereafter.

Our problem is this. Suppose we have to discount this second strand altogether, can the pilgrimage-motif be retained: and even if it can, does it really collapse into a fatuous platitude, a picturesque but unilluminating way of looking at the moral life, without any real imaginative grip? It is fair to suggest that if what I have so far said about moral decision were the whole story, this conclusion would be forced on us. But, fortunately, that oversimplified account needs amending in any case.

[1] The long title of *The Pilgrim's Progress*.

We have spoken as if people opted for a moral code, rather as they might commission a builder to construct a house from a particular architect's plan. In each case, it is implied, we know exactly what we are choosing: we can clearly visualize the finished house, and, in the moral case, we can conceive precisely what it would be like to live in that way. On this account, to realize the chosen way of life may be a strenuous task, but cannot have the spirit of an adventure into unmapped country. We know very well to what we are committing ourselves. Now, this is in fact never our position with regard to any momentous moral choice. We begin with a general and rather empty conception of what we want to achieve—say, a way of life in which love of neighbour is the dominating theme. But what precisely loving one's neighbour is going to amount to, what particular forms it should take in particular situations and with particular neighbours, we do not yet know. How far love involves the vigorous persuading of others to do what one thinks good for them, and how far it involves a near-refusal to manipulate anyone's life, cannot be answered by repeating the slogan 'Love your neighbour', or by referring to a 'parable' (commending love) in which this tricky question is not touched upon. *New* decisions must frequently be made which were never envisaged at an earlier stage in one's moral experience.

Furthermore, the effects of our moral decision on other people and also on ourselves will soon present us with situations very different from those in which our original commitment was made: and it will *go on* constantly changing in ways hard to foresee. That activity of constant adjustment between means and ends, reassessment of policies in the light of unexpected results, the enriching of one's conception of the 'goal', the skimming away of immature, crude elements in one's original idea of it, and the effort to give all this expression in the symbols and parables of which we have spoken—that may reassure us that the ideal of pilgrimage is *not* so foreign to this conception of life as we feared. The metaphor of a changing landscape of pilgrimage, of an obscurely seen destination, a *direction* rather than a clear landmark, the determination not to sit passively under experience as it comes, but to bring it as much as possible into relation (as parable or imaginative slant) with the total vision of life; these fit our outlined secular faith quite as much as they do Christianity. We lose inevitably that strand of meaning in which the pilgrimage of this life reaches its terminus only in the life to come. And this is real loss, without question. But we may still derive from the idea of pilgrimage an over arching, controlling symbol within which all other symbols, myths, and stories can find their setting.

5

The task we set ourselves was twofold: first to inquire whether someone who cannot make sense of the orthodox Christian claims can still give to his life and thought some kind of religious orientation, if he so wishes: and second to discover whether he may continue to enjoy any specifically religious experience (belonging to the content rather than the form of religion) without suspending his disbelief either playfully or disingenuously. Up to this point the first of these problems has been central. The second must be glanced at very briefly, by way of conclusion.

There is not, however, a watertight partition between the two inquiries. The 'sense of pilgrimage', for instance, amounts to more than a merely conceptual framework for moral reflection. It brings to that reflection a quite distinctive *timbre* and feeling-tone, which has already taken us outside the realm of mere form. Also, the idea of an endless approach to an ideal focus, the bringing of more and more of one's experience into relation with that focus, and constantly refining upon the way in which it is symbolized—this idea also gives a place to positive religious attitudes and emotions: reverence for the ideal focus itself and indignation at every idolatry of the second-best.[1]

[1] Here again I am leaning on Professor Findlay's article referred to above, and the ensuing discussion reprinted along with it.

Admitting that great areas of the Christian's religious experience *cannot* be shared by the sceptic at all, it seems to me that one or two quite basic experiences *remain* available to him—perhaps unexpectedly—provided they are reinterpreted along different lines from how the believer takes them. I shall single out one notable example for discussion, the sense of the 'numinous' or holy.

This is the characteristic tone of claimed encounters with deity; the awe of Moses at the burning bush, the Israelites' terror on Mount Sinai; the dread and fascination felt before certain phenomena of nature: it even appears in some of the Romantic poets' response to mountain crag and chasm. The common element in these most varied experiences is what Otto memorably described as the 'numinous'; a stunning, but not horrifying experience, a blend of wonder, ecstasy, and fear at what is too great to be coped with intellectually. It is none of these feelings *exactly*: beyond them all is some element of quite inexpressible strangeness.

Some people possibly never meet this experience, and cannot sympathize imaginatively with those who have. Some meet it only in dreams or under drugs. Others again are haunted by it, awake. Its impact is so compelling and authoritative, that a person who was acquainted with it and who claimed that it disclosed a deity, would suffer immense bewilderment, if he became convinced on independent grounds that such a being does not (or logically could not) exist. His urgent problem would be to know what on earth to 'do about' the experiences to which in his 'believing' period he attached such momentous importance. Are they to be quite discredited as valueless illusions of the senses or imagination? Suppose the Freudians are right and that it is the upsurging of forgotten attitudes and emotions from early childhood which produce this class of experiences through 'projecting' child and parent relations on to the great cinema-screen of nature. What would follow from this? Would the experience, as one suspects, not only have been explained, but also explained *away*? Could it be revived only by temporarily thinking away one's scepticism in a kind of half-hearted, 'let's pretend' game?

In the first place, theologians have been clearly right in insisting that there is something irrational, ultimately non-intellectual, about the experience. It does not yield us any clear concept that entitles us to claim that we have learned something about God: at least not in the way a visit to a zoo can teach us what a tiger or racoon is like. I should want to go further and ask whether numinous awe need necessarily be interpreted as cognitive experience *of* any being at all. And the key word here is 'interpret'. Sense of the numinous does not bring with it its own interpretation. This is the product of reflection about the experience and of the decision about what thought-model will distort it least. To call it ultimately irrational is to confess that no thought-model seems to contain it really neatly. The theists' interpretation can be understood best by imagining a scale that distinguishes different kinds of 'encounter'. At the familiar end of the scale are everyday meetings with men and women in circumstances where they can be seen, heard, touched; or where at least *some* of these checks are possible. Further along, would come those 'intuitions' of presence, the 'hunch' that someone is watching one, or that there is an interloper in a darkened room. Odd as these are, we can check up on them by going on to discover (or not to discover) the suspected persons in the ordinary way. Project this scale beyond all normal experience and beyond all normal tests of verification, and we have the suggestion that the sense of the numinous is in its own way also an intimation of 'presence', though not of the presence of a human being, nor intimated in any understandable fashion.

But this is not the *only* scale on which the numinous could be given a place. We might try, for instance, quite a different one, one we have touched on from time to time in the course of these studies. At one pole we see the natural world as a manipulable tool for satisfying our own wants. We can move away from this view to seeing it as an object of interest in its own right—a problem for intellectual understanding, or an object of aesthetic contemplation. Those experiences of natural beauty which make the strongest impact are those in which nature seems, as it were, to collaborate with the spectator, to take the initiative almost; as when a landscape presents itself as a single, unified 'composition', with a character and 'togetherness' that cannot be analysed simply in terms of its minute ingredients—this clump of trees, this field, that cloud. If we continue the scale in the same direction, it seems as if experiences of the numinous (in nature at any rate) could be shown to lie not far off it. For in these nature is *least of all* seen as a heap of disconnected bits and pieces, awaiting man's exploitation or his rearrangement of them into forms more agreeable to his taste. Nature seems most strongly here to have the initiative, its character to be most nearly personal. But, as on the earlier stages of this scale, the language of 'initiative', 'character', 'personality' can be taken as still the metaphors which they clearly were there. That nature should present itself in this way from time to time is just one more brute fact about it, and indirectly one more brute fact about the man who contemplates it.

This interpretation of the sense of the holy would be quite compatible with the Freudian analysis of religious experience in general. Even in the experience of the numinous, we could say, nature is still being 'manipulated' by man. It is being made the screen on which certain features of his inner life are projected; to repeat the image used earlier. But just as there is a gulf between the ravishing of nature in open-cast mining and the culling of symbols from nature to articulate human thought and feeling (say as Shakespeare culled them), so there is a second gulf between that (largely conscious) symbolizing activity and the quite unconscious modes in which the projecting is accomplished, and human conflicts and reconciliations writ large across the face of nature.

If we regard the ultimate nightmare (from which religion seeks to deliver us) as the failure of all efforts towards 'humanizing' the context of life, a nightmare in which other people are seen only as threats to our own existence, and nature as utterly foreign to us, then we shall still wish to accord a place of importance to numinous and similar experiences, whatever their origin or whatever the mechanism by which they occur. Psycho-analytic explanation degrades those experiences, only so long as they are taken as a sort of knowing or encountering (set on our first scale, that is to say). Taken simply as one way in which our environment can assume a quasi-personal hue, they suffer no devaluation at all.

What kind of reply could one make to the charge that this whole attempt to retain a religious approach to nature is mere fantasy and make-believe, 'subjective' through and through? Its subjectivity is undeniable enough, in the sense that we see nature in the light of our own purposes and commitments. But this is an incomplete answer. It is still a matter for wonderment that nature should *lend* itself as it does to these human activities, should be so malleable to our imagination, that it should 'take' our projections, and (from sometimes unpromising material!) make something so rich and strange out of them. This is a fact of importance about nature itself—one of the many reasons against thinking of it as destructive of, or at least hostile to, all value.

6

We have done no more than begin to open up the problems raised by our two main questions. With regard to the second of them, the question of what specific religious experiences can be still open to the sceptic, we have merely glanced at one instance (although an important one) of how a loss of dogmatic conviction need *not* be as destructive of these as we might have feared. A great deal more detailed work needs to be done here.

Finally, and still more constructively, it should be noticed how certain features of a secular religious orientation can avoid dangers into which religions centred upon a supernatural or transcendent God have frequently fallen. First, it has been stressed through-

out the discussion that the foundations of the whole way of looking at the world and the moral life are those logically underived
moral decisions to follow out a way of life. Since empirical information of all kinds (some of it produced by the special sciences)
can be highly relevant in making up one's mind what way of life
one ought to follow, there can be no science/faith conflict in our
case. Second, although it is hospitable to experiences like the
numinous, it does not interpret them as communications from a
'beyond' concerning how men ought to live. It escapes, therefore,
the risks that go with the claims of prophets and pontiffs to interpret the divine oracle, risks often of intolerance and impatience
with empirically informed opinion, and of shirking the hard work
of investigating the human effects of human policies by resorting
prematurely to the alleged will of God.

The chief value of adding fable, myth, and symbol to moral
judgement is that of enlivening the imagination with memorable
insights into the character of the way of life to which one has
committed oneself. Further, once it is seen clearly how inescapable is *some* imaginative perspective or slant on the non-human
world, commonsense alone would urge the adopting of that slant
that backs up, does not make nonsense of, the value-judgements
one has made. The ceaseless movement towards more adequate
understanding of the ideal (moral and aesthetic), the refinement
of the means of expression, we represented as the movement towards an imaginary focus. From all this it follows that the proper
task of a religious orientation is the *enriching* of life in a great
many different ways. To see this is to see how ridiculous would
be any suggestion that non-religious, unimaginative people who
cannot easily use these aids, should feel guilty or remorseful or
inferior if, *without* them, they can effectively maintain moral
seriousness and achieve integration of character.

INDEX

Index